Irish Sociological Chronicles
volume 1 (1995-96)

ENCOUNTERS WITH MODERN IRELAND

A SOCIOLOGICAL CHRONICLE 1995-1996

Edited by Michel Peillon and Eamonn Slater

IPA

INSTITUTE OF PUBLIC
ADMINISTRATION

First published 1998
by the Institute of Public Administration
57-61 Lansdowne Road
Dublin 4

ISBN 1 872002 59 5

British Library Cataloguing in Publication Data
A catalogue record of this book is available from the British
Library

Cover design by Butler Claffey Design
Origination by Wendy Commins, The Curragh
Printed by Criterion Press, Dublin

Contents

Contributors

Tanya CASSIDY, Trinity College, Dublin

Mary CORCORAN, National University of Ireland, Maynooth

Michele DILLON, Yale University, New Haven, Connecticut

Tom INGLIS, University College Dublin

Carmen KUHLING, University of Limerick

Robbie McVEIGH, Queen's University, Belfast

Patrick O'CARROLL, University College Cork

Barbara O'CONNOR, Dublin City University

Michel PEILLON, National University of Ireland, Maynooth

Emer SHEERIN, National University of Ireland, Maynooth

Eamonn SLATER, National University of Ireland, Maynooth

James WICKHAM, Trinity College, Dublin

Preface

This book has its origin in the conviction that there is room in the public domain for an interesting and relevant sociological voice. And this voice is little heard as yet outside specialised circles. We approached our fellow sociologists and asked them to identify a topic which related to present-day Ireland. We looked for short pieces on events, themes or issues which, they thought, have been particularly relevant during 1995 and 1996. Accordingly, we asked them to provide a short sociological analysis of these issues: that is to say to use a sociological mode of thinking.

We got back a very diverse array of themes and analyses. We soon discovered that although they seemed to be quite different in their subject matter, these contributions did have a common thread running through them: it relates to how Ireland experiences becoming modern. We saw our task as editors to make explicit these common themes by bringing together the articles under a particular heading. In a sense, we have attempted to provide a signposted route to understanding the sociology of modern Ireland.

This represents the first book of a series entitled *Irish Sociological Chronicles*. The next publication in the series will cover 1997-98, and so on. It is anticipated that each volume will become part of a chronicle of on-going sociological commentary on Irish society.

We wish to thank all those who have, in one way or another, contributed to this book. Several organisations have given us permission to reproduce material: The Cork Examiner, Industrial Development Authority, National Road Safety Association. Brigid Corcoran, Kim Slater and Denise Peillon have been generous in allowing us to use their work as illustrations. National University of Ireland, Maynooth has provided a grant to cover part of the cost of printing colour illustrations. Our task was considerably facilitated by the support we received at an early stage from the Publication Committee of the Institute of Public Administration, and especially from Tony MacNamara. Finally, very special thanks are due to all those who have contributed to the text and drawn on their sociological imagination to produce these *Encounters with modern Ireland*.

INTRODUCTION

Becoming an Irish *Flâneur*

EAMONN SLATER

Our project in this work is to introduce you, the reader,
to the sociology of modernity in Ireland. To do this,
we ask you to take on a particular role or perspective
as you read through this book. This imagined role is one of
an urban window shopper, who strolls the streets of a city,
looking at the exotic delights of modern consumer society as
they are displayed in the shop windows. Accordingly, we
present you with a number of windows, each displaying an
aspect of modern Ireland. However, we are not just displaying
these fragments of modern Ireland, we also analyse them in
order to uncover some aspects of the structure of modernity
in Ireland.

The modern stroller: the flâneur

As a way of introducing you to the sociology of modernity, let
us discuss in more detail the role we want you to play as you
gaze at the window displays in this book. The stroller, or
flâneur, has come to hold considerable fascination for the
theorists of modernity. In a sense, this image of an urban
walker has itself become an icon of modernity. The stroll is
now being associated with the way a person experiences and
enjoys the various encounters provided by modern society.
Poets like Baudelaire, cultural critics like Benjamin and

1

sociologists like Simmel have all sought to account for the new experiences of modernity by using the idea of the urban stroller. Charles Baudelaire focused on Paris, while Benjamin and Simmel concentrated on Berlin. For these and for others, the modern city was seen as a site for seeking and experiencing the intoxication of the dream-worlds associated with modern society. And, crucially, these new forms of modernity were to be discovered through walking, through the boulevards and streets of these cities.

It was not just through walking that one enjoyed the sensations of modernity, but significantly through a particular style of walking: strolling. The city offered a site where different kinds of people gathered: where different practices could be witnessed, life-styles sampled. It provided a privileged space for seeking *otherness* in its various forms. And the quest for different ways, different ideas, different peoples and different cultures was done mainly by walking about, without any clear purpose, but with an openness, an availability to whatever may come the way of the stroller. Cities are being increasingly organised for the purpose of strolling, as illustrated by the recent trend to pedestrianise whole districts. They display in shops, department stores and in shopping malls constantly changing exotic images and commodities.

Accordingly, differing ways of walking are directly related to different ways of understanding our immediate surrounds. According to Ann Game,[1] strolling or wandering is to move away from the straight and narrow, and to be led astray by what takes one's fancy. On the other hand, purposeful walking is completely different to strolling as it is concerned with arriving at a particular destination within a particular time frame. Walking to work would be an example of the latter. Strolling has none of these constraining considerations with regard to space and time. The stroll has no concern with a

---

1 Ann Game, *Undoing the social: towards a deconstructive sociology*, Milton Keynes: Open University Press, 1991

2

purposeful end, it is merely interested in distraction and the attraction of the exotic. In following one's sense of curiosity, one is led along an uncharted path. In it, people as well as objects become the focus of the stroller's interest. However, with the emergence of the mass media and increased leisure-time, the dreamworld of modern life has now become part of everyday existence.

The perceived role of the *flâneur* in modern society encapsulates the essential features of modernity. And as the imagery of this modern society has moved away from the physical confines of the street, so has the ability to stroll. We can now "stroll", without the physical constraints of walking, in front of our television sets as we flick through the channels: the ultimate strolling experience! The *flâneur* is the mindset of modernity and therefore the physical embodiment and personification of the forces of modernity within ourselves.

Encountering the themes of Irish modernity

The break away from what can be referred to as the non-modern society has been mainly, but not exclusively, effected through the emergence and development of industrialism. But the modern world follows its own dynamic which leads beyond the industrial society. Such processes are at work in Ireland as elsewhere, and they are now contributing to the shaping of modern Ireland.

Firstly, more and more aspects of society are becoming commodities. Features of industrial society which were out-side the forces of the market are now being incorporated into commodity production. For example, nearly every dimension of popular culture, such as music, dance, intellectual pursuits and even sport, has undergone a process of *commodification*. This process is one of the essential characteristics of modernity. It once marked the break between pre-industrial society and industrial society, and now marks the break between two stages of modern society, between simple and late modernity. Ireland today is very much part of late modernity and seems to have leapfrogged, at least in part, the industrial stage.

The second process at work in the production of modern Ireland is that of *globalisation*. It implies that the distance between Ireland and the outside world is diminishing and that in fact such boundaries are breaking down in many ways. Irish people consume commodities from every possible origin; Irish firms produce commodities and services for every destination. Therefore, Ireland participates in structures which reach far beyond its borders. At the same time as it receives the flows of signs, images and sounds which crisscross the world, it also contributes to them. In such a situation, the whole world is contained within Ireland, and Ireland enjoys direct access to global flows, exchanges and structures.

As the process of commodification penetrates deeper into the cultural realms of society, commodity production takes on a more visual character: this corresponds to a process of *visualisation*. Images and visual symbols become the universal language of commodity production across national boundaries. Television, movies and the advertising industry can replicate images endlessly and beam them virtually everywhere. Featherstone[2] argues that a rapid flow of signs and images now saturates the fabric of everyday life; as a consequence, life has become aestheticised. The *aestheticisation* of everyday life refers to how the boundary between art and everyday life has been effaced. In nearly every aspect of modern society, reproduced imagery plays a role.

Commodities have ceased merely to satisfy needs and they are consumed to signifiy a lifestyle and an identity. But it is not only objects of consumption which carry such meaning. Many activities have been transformed into signs, as elements in the representation and interpretation of the world. Social life increasingly revolves around the communication of such signs, and for that reason culture is becoming central to society, as the flows of symbols, images, information and signs

---

2 Mike Featherstone, "Postmodernism and the aesthecization of everyday life", in Scott Lash and Jonathan Friedman (eds), *Modernity and identity*, Oxford: Blackwell, 1992, pp 265-90

spread to many areas of everyday life. This is the modern *process of signification*.

All the processes which have promoted and ushered in modern society have broken a magic spell: the spell of simply belonging to a very definite and familiar social world, a world which we took for granted. The growth of the city, literacy and communication, industrial production have brought people into contact with different values, life-styles, and above all with the possibility of change and progress in one's own social conditions. The *pluralism* of modern society exposes us to a range of diverse experiences, thrusting upon us the awareness of a plural world. Things are different elsewhere and could be different here. We are now faced with a range of alternatives. And this process is nowadays acquiring greater intensity and greater urgency. According to Anthony Giddens,[3] in "high modernity" most aspects of social activity are revised in the light of new information or knowledge and social practices are constantly examined accordingly, subjected to critical review. *Reflexivity*, now a central feature of social life, refers to the fact that individuals, groups and institutions proceed in a self-conscious way, that they reflect on their activity. This passage from taken-for-granted attitudes to monitoring had already marked the passage from the traditional to the modern world. But this reflexive monitoring of social practices becomes more crucial in the latest phase of modern life. So much so that modernity institutionalises doubt.

The idea of social differentiation has deep roots in the history of social thinking. It refers to the process through which societies become more complex and diverse. At the end of this process we have, we are told, the modern society which is characterised by pluralism. Different aspects of social life acquire their own features and impetus. Now only loosely connected, these aspects operate according to their own rules.

---

3 Anthony Giddens, *The consequences of modernity*, Cambridge: Polity Press, 1990

Such *fragmentation* points to the potentially contradictory or chaotic character of modern society; for such differing elements do not easily coexist.

Modernity has been presented as enlightenment and progress. But it was not long before it revealed its dark side. By perceiving itself as progressing, and on the right side of history, modern society set out to realise whatever model of the good society it defined for itself. Those who do not conform to this project are rather ruthlessly marginalised and, if possible, eliminated. Upholders of unorthodox lifestyles, such as nomads or members of subcultural communes, but also people who, like small farmers, are deemed to have little to offer modernity, meet such a fate of *marginalisation* and *intolerance*. Not everything goes in a modern society and pluralism possesses definite limits. It produces its own boundaries and endeavours to reject into a shadowy margin that which does not comfortably take its place within the modern order. But it meets resistance in doing so.

Signposts

Those are the main encounters that modern Ireland offers to the *flâneur* within it. You may only get a glimpse of such processes, for they rarely manifest themselves on their own. In an attempt to make sense of the diversity inherent in modern society, we use four main signposts in this text to guide you towards such encounters. These signposts point to significant aspects of present-day Ireland:

    (1) Images for sale
    (2) Signs of the time
    (3) Reflexivity
    (4) Limits to modernity

In continuing the metaphor of the *flâneur*, these signposts will act as street names in our stroll along the shop fronts of Irish society. They will guide you to the very points where the processes which have been identified previously manifest themselves, sometimes on their own, other times combined with other processes.

IMAGES FOR SALE

... consuming Temple Bar

CHAPTER 1

The Re-enchantment of Temple Bar

MARY CORCORAN

Temple Bar is a geographically demarcated entity, a tax designated area, an archaeological site, a centre for culture and the arts, a tourist attraction, a building site. Temple Bar has become synonymous with the concept of urban renewal and also functions as a metaphor for cultural renaissance. Yet a little over ten years ago it was just another run-down street in a forgotten part of Dublin. How and why was this transformation from *no place* to *some place* effected? To answer this question requires an examination of the cultural and economic contexts within which Temple Bar has been conceived and developed. I will argue that the Temple Bar urban renewal scheme reveals an inextricable linkage between culture and commerce played out in a discourse which privileges the powerful and marginalises the vernacular in human terms, *and* in terms of the landscape.

History and identity

Dublin's attempt in recent years to reinvent itself is part of a general effort by older cities to liberate themselves from their ageing industrial past and generate a new and, crucially, *more marketable* identity. Temple Bar is the story of one such re-invention. Temple Bar is a historical area of central Dublin which was earmarked by CIE (Córas Iompar Éireann) in the

1970s as a possible site for a downtown transportation depot. CIE accumulated a large property portfolio in the area and, while awaiting the finalisation of the redevelopment plans, rented buildings on short-term leases. Very quickly, an indigenous community of artists, bohemians and small business owners took up residence in the area, which offered spaces and places for the development of a broad range of arts and cultural activities, and alternative outlets. A tenant group and An Taisce (the National Trust of Ireland) joined forces to oppose CIE's development plan, and their actions eventually brought about a change of heart among policy-makers about the potential use of Temple Bar. In 1991, both national and local government committed themselves to the preservation of the Temple Bar area and its redevelopment as a distinctive cultural quarter in the capital. The area has now entered a second phase of redevelopement under a Framework Plan largely driven by tax-incentives, and administered by a development corporation, Temple Bar Properties Ltd.

Temple Bar has been symbolically constructed in the public's imagination as a cultural or *Latin quarter* and as Dublin's own *left bank*. In reality, however, the area has been domesticated, packaged and themed so that it now constitutes a key segment in Dublin Tourism's tourist trail. While Temple Bar markets itself as a state-of-the-art cultural centre, it is primarily driven by a "bums on seats" (or punters in the streets) economic logic. On one level, Temple Bar represents the artistic and architectural aspirations of Dublin's cultural cognoscenti. But on an altogether more banal level, it works as a mini-theme-park processing punters through purpose-designed eating establishments and public houses, playing host to what one journalist recently described as "drunken stag parties, lost tourists, gangs of teenagers, and out-of-tune buskers singing Oasis numbers".[1]

Temple Bar's mandate was to develop a vibrant city

---

1 Linda Higgins, "The quay to happiness", in *Irish Independent, Dubliners Supplement*, January 14, 1997

precinct characterised by a mix of residential, business and cultural uses in keeping with the existing profile of the area, and exciting enough to attract significant numbers of visitors. While there is no doubt that Temple Bar does attract visitors, it is questionable whether the development that has occurred has fulfilled the original remit. Some of the original tenants now look out of place rather than at home in the *new look* Temple Bar.

Square Wheel Cycle Works

Square Wheel Cycleworks has been running a cycle shop and parking service since the early 1980s in Temple Bar. Then, it was a stopping-off place before heading uptown to Grafton Street, or downtown to Henry Street. Now it is a reminder of the colourful shabbiness of a district which is undergoing substantial face-lifting. The bohemian ambience of the Progressive Cafe or the bric-a-brac Tambuli outlet seem increasingly anomalous as the heart of Temple Bar is realigned along a cultural/commercial nexus. Eating out in Temple Bar has become an eclectic past-time, and shopping has become chic. The vernacular, or local character of the landscape, has ceded to the opaque forces of commercialism. The opacity of the commercial logic at work in Temple Bar arises from the artistic and cultural mantle which has been assumed by the urban renewal project since its inception.

Progressive Cafe

The marriage of culture and commerce

There is a growing sociological literature on the close relationship, in the period of late industrialism, between capital accumulation (a market-oriented and profit-driven strategy) and cultural consumption. Urban revitalisation which involves the linking of an accumulation strategy with a cultural policy, amounts to the operation of what has been termed an *artistic mode of production*.[2] In other words, the production, distribution and consumption of arts and culture operate as a cover for capitalist expansion. In the case of Temple Bar, the adaptation of an artistic mode of production grew indirectly from the opposition of An Taisce and the indigenous artistic community to CIE's strategy for urban renewal. Given the shortage of sites for redevelopment in the central city and the highly attractive tax incentive package made available for development in Temple Bar, developers were easily attracted to the area. The arts and artistic preservation provided a convenient marker to which the redevelopment strategy could be tagged. Ironically, the artists who developed the initial beachhead in Temple Bar activated a mechanism of revalorisation that ultimately had the effect of destabilising the existing uses and markets in the area. Many of the original tenants can no longer afford the rents in Temple Bar, and have been displaced across the Liffey into the Ormond Multi-Media Centre on the North Quays. The artistic mode of production fundamentally is driven not just by culture but by economic incentives and, in particular, the capitalist propensity for accumulation. Development in Temple Bar has been extremely capital intensive. According to the *Development Programme for Temple Bar*, total investment in the area between 1991-1999 will amount to IR£200 millions. In addition, apart from the cultural quarter, the emphasis is on individualised rather than socialised consumption. In other words, development in the area is oriented toward a particular type of consumer: the young, single, high-earning resident or visitor. In terms of housing allocation, for example, all of the residential units built so far have been in the private sector, and have been marketed at investors or a professionalised middle class. There are plans in the pipeline to construct social housing in West Temple Bar, but those homes will be reserved

---

2 Sharon Zukin, *Loft living: culture and capital in urban change*, Baltimore, MD: Johns Hopkins University Press, 1982, p 176

exclusively for senior citizens, a group hardly likely to lower the tone of the neighbourhood. The proliferation of pubs, bars, coffee shops, hotels, and special interest shops and boutiques in the area attests to the way in which Temple Bar is as much in thrall to the culture of consumption as to the consumption of culture. Arts and culture lend themselves as mechanisms through which a revalorisation of the urban may occur.

In the development and design of Dublin's cultural quarter, a concerted attempt has been made to appropriate both the authenticity of the past *and* the uniqueness of the new, an approach which replicates other urban renewal schemes in Europe and the United States. The employment of key strategies in the area development plan set the scene for the *re-enchantment of Temple Bar*. Robins[3] identifies a number of mechanisms through which cities may seek to re-invent themselves: the restoration of a pre-modern sense of place and tradition, the invocation of state of the art technology in an attempt to create a postmodern, electronic garden city, and the marketing of the *re-imaged* city to potential con-sumers. It is useful to think about these re-enchantment strategies in the context of Temple Bar's remarkable incarnation as a cultural quarter in the recent past.

The essential authenticity of Temple Bar derives from its history, albeit a reconstructed one. The neighbourhood, which only acquired the designation "Temple Bar" when concerned members of An Taisce leapt to its defence in the mid-nineteen eighties, has been in existence for well over two hundred years. Excavations that preceded urban redevelopment have revealed the architectural richness of the area, including the remains of the Viking settlement of Dublin. This historical legacy is reproduced for the late twentieth century consumer in the form of a Viking Adventure multi-media presentation developed for Dublin Tourism, and the exhibition of artifacts

---

3   Kevin Robins, "Prisoners of the city", in E. Carter *et al.* (eds), *Space and place: theories of identity and location*, London: Lawrence and Wishart, 1993, pp 304-06

in dedicated areas within Temple Bar. The past has been neatly sifted from the earth, retrieved, catalogued, conserved and made presentable. Thus, Temple Bar has become an integral part of the heritage industry which has been popularised in Irish tourism policy in recent years.

In an attempt at historical revivalism, the Temple Bar Development Plan placed enormous emphasis on refurbishing and retaining buildings of listed historical interest. As An Taisce has pointed out, this did not prevent the demolition of numerous buildings of character and distinction, and the destructive treatment of others. However, the retention of many building facades and the creative refurbishment of a few, has ensured that Temple Bar at least retains a *historical veneer*. Much was made of the conservation of the former Presbyterian Meeting House on Eustace Street, which is now a Cultural Centre for Children (the Ark). In actual fact, the only part of the original eighteenth century building

The Ark

retained for the Ark was the front wall. Most of the original features of the building which had survived conversion to warehousing use were demolished. The building has been completely reconstructed from within to accommodate an artistic programme for children.

Coupled with the partial attempt at preservation, there has been an equally remarkable attempt at architectural innovation in Temple Bar. At an early stage in the development process, it was decided that Temple Bar needed a flagship project to give the area a distinctive identity. That project was to be the arts and culture. Accordingly, a series of existing buildings were refurbished and new buildings were commissioned to house cultural and artistic activities.

The core of Dublin's cultural quarter is centred on Meeting House Square, which now houses the Gallery of Photography, the National Photographic Archive, the Gaiety School of Acting, the Dublin Institute of Technology's School of Photography and the Irish Film Centre. These buildings follow an introverted layout in that they are positioned around a central square or piazza which can be accessed through three restricted points.

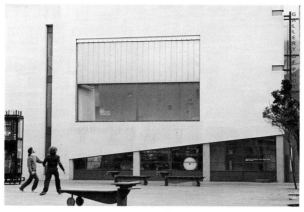

Gallery of Photography, Meeting House Square

Along Curved Street, leading towards Meeting House Square, are housed Music Base and the ArtHouse, the multi-media Centre for the Arts. According to publicity material, ArtHouse is a centre for the arts which bridges art and technology. ArtHouse seeks to ensure that new technologies are used to best advantage by the cultural sector to reach a wider audience. How this is made possible in practice is not clear. Indeed, at the 1997 Architectural Association of Ireland's annual awards, ArtHouse presented as something of a puzzle to the assessors who expressed doubts about what actually goes on there. It would appear, however, that at least the availability of multi-media technology allows for the constitution of electronically linked communities of artists and cultural workers who are not place bound. In this sense, the development of ArtHouse is avant-garde, contrasting with the counter focus elsewhere in Temple Bar's development plan on the retention of authenticity.

From its inception, Temple Bar Properties Ltd embarked on an ambitious marketing plan. A key part of the overall marketing strategy was to establish a distinct locational identity for the area as a vibrant and exciting cultural quarter. This was achieved through advertising and media campaigns at national and international levels. Great emphasis has been placed in Temple Bar's promotional literature on the increasing number of resident and visiting consumers in the area.

Gentrification

The *artistic mode of production*, in which the arts and culture are harnessed in the interests of commercialism, may be seen as a response to the greater availability of leisure time and more *sophisticated* patterns of consumption in advanced industrial society. Changing patterns of consumption have engendered a process of gentrification in which older, decaying parts of the urban fabric are revalorised economically and aesthetically. Gentrification creates a situation in which the vernacular or authentic core of older – usually rundown

– neighbourhoods are restylised as landscape and invested with cultural power.[4] In the case of Temple Bar, developers, attracted by generous tax incentives made available by the government, embarked on refurbishment and new construction projects. The limited housing stock in the area has been sought after primarily by higher earning professionals. Apartment prices reflect the superior profile of the Temple Bar area which has been greatly enhanced by a massive public capital infusion and the area's growing cultural cachet. Apartment prices and rents are significantly lower on the North City quays. Temple Bar has taken on an aesthetic value which is convertible into monetary terms. Gentrification is made possible because a critical mass of high-earning professionals are prepared to pay for the privilege of living, eating or shopping in Temple Bar.

In Temple Bar, culture and commerce coalesce into something part real, part pastiche. Conservation, refurbishment and redevelopment often leave buildings with the appearance of antiquity, while masking the wholesale evisceration of the original which has occurred within. The *artistic mode of production* makes it possible to appropriate buildings from their original functional context, and refashion them as picturesque emporiums for consumption. This is made politically acceptable by emphasising a conservation agenda.

A perusal of the Temple Bar area reveals a proliferation of boutiques and services which are directed at a key market segment, the urban gentry or upmarket professionals with disposable incomes. The Design Yard is represented in Temple Bar's cultural discourse (and no doubt in their marketing strategy) as a centre of excellence in the field of contemporary applied arts. The Design Yard is housed in a modern conversion of an eighteenth century warehouse. It is quintessentially postmodern in the sense that the building has been abstracted from its mercantile capitalist origins –

---

4   Jane Jacobs, "Cultures of the past and urban transformation", in
    K. Anderson and F. Gale (eds), *Inventing places*, Melbourne: Long-
    man Cheshire, 1992, p 196

Design Yard

as a warehouse – and renewed as an up to date emporium behind the grey brick facade of the past. It is a monument to consumption in that it exhibits and sells expensive jewellery and customised furniture, ceramic and glass products, lighting and textiles. Further along East Essex Street is the entrance to the refurbished Clarence Hotel, whose Scandinavian inspired, minimalist decor has been eulogised in the style press. In terms of aesthetic taste and style, the Clarence has achieved iconic status. Before refurbishment, this hotel was traditionally a hostelry for country people visiting Dublin. As such, it formed part of the local vernacular. Redevelopment has transformed the Clarence into an ultra-chic sanctuary for the rich and famous. After all, it is owned by the internationally famous rock group, U2. In the quaintly named Tea Rooms restaurant – resonant of the hotel's past – gourmet food is served to an urban gentry. The traditional clientele, rural visitors to the city, have been displaced. The

About Face

Cyberia

Clarence, which occupied a particular identity within the vernacular of Dublin City's quays, has been effectively reconstituted as landscape, and invested with cultural power.

A couple of blocks away, a restored brick-fronted building houses About Face, a specialist boutique for men's skincare and aftershave products. After a relaxing facial, one may retire to the Cyberia Cafe, housed in the ArtHouse, to drink coffee and surf the Internet. The frontage of the Cyberia Cafe inverts that of the traditional coffee shop. In name (Siberia) and in countenance it is cold and clinical, minimalist in design and unwelcoming in ambience. The same could be said of Meeting House Square, whose introverted nature creates not the air of a piazza but of a cold, and permanently shaded chamber. As one local resident quipped, "it's the hospital that Tallaght never got".

Unusually for a public square, Meeting House Square has been, until recently, off limits to the public after 6:00 in the evening. Its opening hours have been extended to accommodate a new restaurant, but the square is now under the

Public seating in Meeting House Square

The Auld Dubliner

surveillance of security cameras and a night watchman. This reflects a general preoccupation with security in Temple Bar, to protect against unwelcome interlopers. The number of residents has increased from two hundred to just under one thousand since the inception of the project. All are housed in relatively upmarket private residential developments. A community joint initiative, highlighted in the *Development Programme for Temple Bar*, lists the establishment of a community based security plan with the Department of Justice and Garda Siochana, comprising a Businesswatch scheme, a dedicated community garda force and closed circuit TV for public spaces. Thus the residents of Temple Bar live in a virtual gated community.

Traversing the streets of Temple Bar, one experiences a disturbing impression of a wholesale evisceration in progress. The streets are furnished with skips and scaffolding. The area is peopled by construction workers. Buildings are razed to the ground from within, their exteriors retaining the pre-

Flannerys Temple Bar

tence that all is not changed. It is a place begun, but unfinished. But in its incompleteness, we are exposed to the remaking of authenticity and the redundancy of the real. Before it obtained its current status as a designated cultural quarter, Temple Bar was home to three traditional Dublin pubs: The Auld Dubliner, The Norseman and Flannery's (Temple Bar). The Norseman has had its exterior refashioned so that it is now virtually indistinguishable from the formula pubs that have colonised suburbia in recent years. The Auld Dubliner and Flannery's have been reduced to empty shells and restructured from within.

These public bars, which conferred on the area its slightly scruffy, bohemian air, have ceased to exist in space and time. In their new incarnations as "booze barns", they are facelifted and soulless. A revitalisation project that was begun with the expressed mission of building on the existing distinctiveness of the area, has taken that which was distinct – the spit and sawdust bar – and sanitised it so that it is now little more than a trendy parody of its former self.

If, as I have argued, place and landscape are socially constructed, in whose interests has Temple Bar been re-imaged, and re-made? While the re-enchantment of Temple Bar proceeds apace, inner-city communities in Dublin and elsewhere raise their voices in a chorus of dis-enchantment. They bear witness to the destruction of their neighbourhoods by drugs, unemployment and social deprivation. The vast majority of people in deprived communities throughout the country will never attend, much less participate, in an arts or cultural event. Yet substantial amounts of public funding have been used to underwrite the creation of a *cultural quarter* in Temple Bar. But Temple Bar is not about making arts and culture more accessible to the community-at-large. Rather Temple Bar is about harnessing the twin motifs of arts and culture in the interests of capitalist development. In reality, Temple Bar is now closer to Eurodisney than Paris-on-the-Liffey. The bohemianism which gave Temple Bar its name has been appropriated and restyled into something safer, more homogenous and consumer-friendly. In that process, the vernacular, or local character of the area has been marginalised.

... the eye deceived ...

CHAPTER 2

The Lure of Colour

EAMONN SLATER

This year we have reached another threshold in the evolution of our society; for the first time in our history we will have had more visitors coming to our country than we have permanent residents here. This massive influx of tourists is having a number of effects on our economy and on our society. Some of these are obvious, such as more money, more jobs and more contact with other peoples of the globe. But there are other features of this tourist wave which seem to be ignored, little discussed and in many cases not even recognised as being emerging features of modern Irish society. One such feature is our current trend of *doing up* our town-scapes and villagescapes in order to make them look more charming and more appealing for our visitors.

A peacock plumage of colour

This self-conscious image improvement scheme began a number of years ago with the Tidy Town competition, but recently we seem to be moving into a new phase of townscape *face-lifting*, one which is characterised by an extravaganza of brightly painted buildings, displaying a great variety of vivid and outrageous colours. Accordingly, the typical grey skies of the West now stand in contrast to a seemingly unending spectrum of colours. Such an extravaganza of colour, for

example, is displayed by the village of Eyeries on the Beara peninsula in County Cork.

Here we see how each building, private and commercial, has established its own individual difference from its immediate neighbours by displaying a contrasting splash of colour. In consequence, the whole row of buildings form a peacock-like plumage of red, blue, pink and green. As can be seen, this ostentatious display is *backgrounded* by a band of grey clouds on the surrounding mountain tops. The freshly painted buildings of Eyeries and other villages like it are now acting as a visual antidote to the typical greyness of the West. And in doing so, establishing themselves as oases of colour in a desert of dull greyness. What one is seeing is not the normal display of urban colour, all too evident in cities or in suburbia in general. These urban scapes are usually characterised by their dullness, their uniform lack of colour and are consequently far removed along the colour spectrum from this West of Ireland *peacock* of Eyeries. According to John Urry, a well-known sociologist of tourism, this contrast is not an accident, but a planned strategy on behalf of local communities to attract tourists. Urry[1] has argued that tourism

1 John Urry, "The Consumption of tourism", *Sociology*, vol 24 (1990): 23-35

is essentially about gazing upon exotic scapes, including both landscapes and townscapes. As objects of the gaze they have to be exotic because, for Urry, the tourist practice is one of *departure* from the practices of everyday life and, crucially, from the physical environment of the urban workplace and the housing estates of suburbia. Therefore, the vividly exciting facades of Eyeries create a set of visual stimuli to the visiting tourists that attempts to distract their attention away from the modern urban world and in doing so hopefully away from the social and personal problems associated with that built world.

By being forced to gaze upon a physically contrasting environment, the visitors may also begin to contemplate the possibility of another world (without the problems of urban modernity), a world residing behind the vibrant facades of these streetscapes. This idea of a non-urban arcadia is suggested by the possibility that the facades are actually reflecting the presence of an exotic people within, who with their cheerful and gaily painted exteriors give off the impression that they themselves may have similar personality traits. However, this is a hopeless prospect and a useless daydream. When the whole street takes on this type of appearance, it is

likely the consequence of an orchestrated effort on behalf of the community as a whole rather than the personal whim of each and every resident of the street. In summary, the street display of colour is closer to a staged film set than it is to a personal expression of exuberance. You certainly get this staging effect when you turn to descend the hill in Eyeries and you are presented with the panoramic view of its main street (see photo, page 41).

Again, you can see a long sweep of contrasting colours running from the red-painted building in the foreground to the pale green facade in the distance. This streetscape is painted exotically in order to attract the tourists into it. But if this view and the other constructed ones are going to work as a luring mechanism, they must excite the curiosity of the passer-by. In modern Ireland this usually means travellers touring by car. And because of the inherent rapidity of movement associated with the car, the visual lures used must be extremely impressive. The more flamboyant the visual display the greater is the tendency to attract the attention of the car occupiers, hence the importance of vivid colours. If the initial glance is also a panoramic one, where the whole village or at least most of it can be seen from one commanding vantage point, this intensifies the quaintness to be experience. Therefore, a clear uninterrupted view of the streetscape is essential to create this collective sense of quaintness. One highly decorated building in itself will not be able to define the whole village as quaint or charming. So a long sweeping view of cheerfully coloured buildings is necessary, if the passing tourists are going to be lured from their cars onto these *streets of desire*.

The visual disharmony of dereliction

But a sweeping view of exotic quaintness is not that easy to construct. Any visual disharmony in the scene will destroy the whole constructed sense of harmony of the place and accordingly undermine the collective effort to achieve the staged appearance of quaintness. A non-cooperating neighbour or, more significantly, the absence of one – a situation which could physically reveal itself in a derelict building or site in the street – could potentially destroy the attempted picture-postcard view. Accordingly, the local village community needs to develop strategies to combat these forces of destruction, forces which are not only social, i.e. unoccupied premises, but also natural, i.e. decay. When a building is *let go*, these two forces of destruction can form a formidable combination to test the resolve of any community. The type of strategy adopted to counteract the visually displeasing depends on the level of dereliction the community has to deal with. An attempt at restoration was undertaken by the residents of Eyeries on main street, which we have seen in the last photograph. Because this effort was not visibly obvious in the photograph, it must be considered a success. However, a closer look at the red building on the left reveals how this visual quaintness was maintained by the village community.

From the photograph it is clear that there is something odd about the appearance of this facade. Firstly, its walls have been painted a flaming red and this has been done fairly recently because the paint still retains its sheen. But its windows *paint* a different picture, one of destruction. A number of the glass panes have been broken and have been replaced with crude wooden panels. However, what is significant about this repair job is how it was done. The repairs were made from the outside of the building, indicating that it was *repaired* by a person who did not have access to the premises. Unoccupied, the house remains extremely prone to both the social and natural forces of decay. Happily for the local community, this building is at the first stage of dereliction only and it may be possible to reverse the decaying process by getting someone to take up residence again in the near future. At the moment, a holding job has to do, i.e. holding its appearance in order to give the impression that it is occupied by a *cheerful* resident. But at the other end of Eyeries, the process of dereliction has run its full course.

Here, we see a huge gaping hole in the sweep of the street – a coat of paint is useless because there is nothing left to hang that coat on. In this situation, as the gap in the streetscape cannot be hidden, it must be used to create a different sense of quaintness and streetscape exoticism. Since dereliction and decay signify destruction and disorder in both the natural and man-made worlds, if this process is to be reversed or even rectified, some sort of order has to be re-imposed on the site. In the photograph one can see how the rubble has been removed and the ground levelled and planted with grass. This restoration of order over the site is extended by the architectural use of the straight edge, graphically illustrated by the raised edge of the foot-path and the sitting area. The imposed order of the straight edging is further enhanced by the way in which the actual backdrop is framed between the gable walls of the adjoining buildings and by the retention of a low back wall. Not only has the surrounding country landscape been allowed to enter into the townscape, but this has been done in such a way as to give the impression of being framed in a picture-like structure between the straight edges of the remaining walls. The natural landscape of the surrounding countryside has been *framed* in the streetscape in such a way as to make it look as if it is an image on a wall rather than a gap between two walls. And as if to complete this process of re-enchantment of the scape, a mural is painted on one of the walls, depicting a local scene associated with the mythical story of the "Hag of Beara". What is interesting about this mural is that its painted horizon nearly matches the real horizon out on the sea. But this possible blurring of the world of art and the real world does not stop here; across the street from this idyllic scene there stands a building, which has the appearance of a house? But is it a house?

The optical illusion of trompe-l'œil

The orange coloured building shown in the photo below (page 46) looks a little the worst for wear, as indicated by the peeling of paint from the wall. However, unlike the red-painted building on main street, the window panes here look intact and there is some evidence that the house is lived in, as suggested by what looks like lace curtains in the ground-floor window. But this is, in fact, the most compelling optical

illusion in the village of Eyeries. When one pulls back and takes a side view of the building, one discovers that its roof has long since collapsed and it is unoccupied.

From the side angle below, we see immediately that we have been tricked into believing that this derelict building is a cosy home. How was this illusion performed on us? By the use of paint and the artful technique of *trompe-l'œil. Trompe-*

l'œil roughly translates as the "eye deceived".[2] In this style of painting, the artist is able to give a two-dimensional picture the semblance of a three-dimensional world. In the photograph, the windows and the door are not real doors or windows but mere representations of them. They are actually images painted onto flat wooden surfaces, where the real objects should be. In order for this visual gag to work, the paintings of the objects must fit perfectly into the setting (or surroundings) in which the real objects would have existed. Therefore, as a construct, this building is closer to the world of art than to the real world of everyday life.

Trompe-l'œil is the pinnacle of optical illusion within the world of art. Because of that it possesses a certain charm about it which ideally suits it to the function of a luring mechanism: the luring of tourists into the villages of Ireland. Essentially, it nurtures a gaze of long duration. The initial glance tends to accept the appearance presented to the eye, even if something odd or unusal appears to be present. A second glance is necessary in order to absorb the oddity perceived in the first glance. In this one, the spectator usually discovers that he/she has been the victim of a hoax, a visual hoax. But the lure of *trompe-l'œil* does not stop there. The next stage of this extended gaze is the effort to discover how the hoax was perpetrated in the first place. This heightened curiosity generally compels the spectator to get as close to the painting as possible so that she/he can reach out and touch the surface of the painting rather than the real objects it represents. The spectator is compelled to move physically closer to the artful structure; such movement reveals how this type of constructed gaze is probably the most engaging of all gazes, the ultimate luring device.

The whole villagescape of Eyeries is actually a form of *trompe l'œil*, in the sense that various art forms and techniques are used to lure the tourists into its precincts. The re-

---

2   Miriam Milman, *Trompe l'œil painting: the illusion of reality,* London: Macmillan, 1982

enchantment of the physical place is achieved by painting the facades of the buildings in order to give the impression of cheerfulness and gaiety. But the process of re-enchantment is not just about the aesthetic experience of the villagescape, it also has an economic and social dimension to it. In staging the appearance of cosy street homes, occupied by locals, the village community is actually hiding the reality of its own underpopulation. It is underpopulated in the sense that there is not a sufficient population of residents to occupy all the street houses and thereby maintain a complete streetscape. Therefore, art and its inherent illusion comes into play as a means of not only attracting the tourists in, but also of deceiving them and others that all is gaiety and cheerfulness in this picturesque village, when the reality is quite different, i.e. one of struggle to survive economically. This visual act of deception is not determined by any explicit desire of the local community to deceive, but is a direct consequence of using art to lure tourists. In attempting to attract the tourists to it, the village of Eyeries has re-imaged itself to look quaint and charming to the outsider, but in doing so it has straight-jacketed itself into an identity, an identity created for cultural consumption by others. Eyeries along with other such villages in the West of Ireland has remained remote and under-developed; it is experiencing decline. Nonetheless, it is trying to survive, by using the enhanced physical appearance as a way of promoting its economic performance. The West is attempting to stay awake by the lure of colour!

... cultural pointers

CHAPTER 3

Heritage Centres

EMER SHEERIN

Heritage has become one of the soundbites of the 90s. It is associated with theme parks, interpretive centres, rural and urban renewal and, crucially, with tourism. And as an idea in the public arena, it has stimulated interest in a number of areas of modern society: the interpretation of the past, the recontruction of the past, the democratisation of the past, the notion of a sense of place and the appreciation of landscape, as well as issues of community and national identities.

In order to understand the nature of heritage I want to argue that we need to see how it is inextricably linked with the tourist industry. Heritage has emerged as an economic resource. A country's heritage has become its tourism *product*: a commodity to be marketed, packaged and sold to visitors. Thus there is a consumer-driven approach to the business of heritage, to its interpretation, to its representation of the past.

Contested heritage

This notion of viewing heritage as an economic resource has given rise to much debate in the media in recent years. One of the hottest controversies in this country surrounds the location of interpretive centres and national parks. The physical siting of proposed national parks, for example in the Burren region and in the Wicklow mountains, has stimulated much heated discussion. Opponents perceive them as intrusive and destructive, while their supporters see them as potential providers of employment and as opportunities for enhancing these less developed regions.

Other contentious issues in the area of heritage concern the degree of local involvement in representations of the past in heritage centres, with important decisions on local history being taken by so-called professionals in the heritage and tourism industries. These new heritage professionals have accordingly diminished the role of the more traditional interpreters of our past – the historians and archaeologists.

Heritage also gives rise to concern regarding the educational value of heritage interpretation and the heightened importance of entertainment, providing pleasurable experiences to visitors to heritage sites. Here, the notion of *authenticity* is a vital issue to the whole debate. This debate revolves around the apparent contradiction in the attempt to provide an entertaining experience and an authentic representation of the past at the same time.

In a country with a heritage as rich and varied as Ireland, and with an increasing reliance on the tourism industry, these issues are very topical of late. According to the latest survey, there are one hundred and forty-eight heritage-based tourist attractions in Ireland. These can be divided into five main types: historic houses and castles; interpretive centres, museums and folk parks; nature and wildlife parks; historic monuments; heritage gardens.

Let us now take a look at the notion of heritage in the context of its being a direct product of the tourist industry in modern Ireland, showing in particular how this link has affected our representations of the past.

The museum

Central to the notion of heritage is the act of representing the past. By looking at the methods of representing the past in museums of the nineteenth century, we will have a yardstick to measure changes in the regimes of representation in the modern heritage centres. In the museums of the nineteenth century, culture came to be thought of as a resource for a more effective form of social management. Promoting acceptable norms of behaviour could proceed, it was thought, by exposing the public to a more *cultured* environment.[1] For example, it was no accident that museum exhibits were put into large palladian buildings like the National Museum in Kildare street. Upon entering the majestic doorways of this building, the spectator was and is compelled by the architectural splendour to maintain a respectful silence in front of a reconstructed past. The museum was thus essentially about the instruction and edification of the general public.

The modes of representing the past in such museums were therefore very much a reflection of the nineteenth century society. In essence, curators were opening up private collections to the public. The old Modernist thinking on advancement and progress towards the ever more modern world was paralleled in the display of objects in the museum's exhibits, in which real artifacts and objects were ordered and named within frameworks of evolution. As a mode of representation, therefore, the museum inherently supported the status quo. The museum's *system of objects* enabled it to endow the artefact with new meaning to support the museum's own vision of history, replacing its historical and social context with new artistic and aesthetic categories in which the aura of the object was enhanced. The museums of the nineteenth century were very much a reflection of the social and cultural forces of that time.

The heritage centre

The modes of representation in the heritage centre differ from that of the traditional museum. These modes can be

1 Tony Bennett, *The birth of the museum,* London: Routledge, 1995

summarised as the process of visualisation. In this process the past is activated by visual witnessing through the use of modern technology. With the help of advancements in the technology of replication, the image becomes central to the heritage centre. The image, which may be created through a variety of different media, helps the visitor to visualise life patterns or events from times past. In the traditional museum, it was necessary to display a real artifact or object in order to represent the past, but in the heritage centre, a reproduced image will fulfill the same function. It is the image, moving or still, which commands the dominant position in the heritage centre's presentation, enabling visitors to witness an event from the past through their own eyes, immediately.

In this process of representation, the visual is dominant over the verbal. This causes visitors to view the image or the real artefact first. This is because the moving or still image – the photography, the audio-visual display or the real object itself – tends to focus the attention of the visitor initially, before he or she goes on to read the written caption which usually accompanies the visual display. In this light, the verbal narrative is still a vital component of the visualisation process. The narrative structure involves providing the visitor with an acceptable interpretation of the image displayed. An image in itself cannot tell its own story, it needs a verbal caption to do so. The narrative provides explanation and interpretation of what has been witnessed in the image.

Simulation is another important element in the visualis-ation process. Here the heritage centre employs actor-interpreters who are trained to speak in dialects existing in the particular era or area which is the subject of the exhi-bition. Bunratty Folk park is Ireland's most famous example of constructed simulation. Here, the process of simulation is enhanced by a number of reconstructed elements which appeal to our senses, reconstructed traditional townscapes, tastes, smells and rural sounds. Such forms of simulation, aided by electronic media, render the heritage centre's display as seemingly natural and real.

The representation of Ireland according to visual categories, however, is deeply rooted in pre-existing regimes of representation. This can be seen in depictions of the Irish landscape which highlight Ireland's long history of picturesque representations. These began with English travellers representing Ireland according to their own preconceived notions: a very selective and exclusively aesthetic representation of Ireland. Such depictions demonstrated an awareness of the *otherness* of Ireland and illustrated the nature of the ongoing relationship between England and Ireland as one consequent upon relations between the coloniser and the colonised. The purely aesthetic nature of the picturesque representations enabled the visitors to ignore certain important aspects of Irish life such as poverty and conflict which were a major feature of life throughout the country at the time. This pursuit of the picturesque may be seen as the origin of touristic endeavour in Ireland, in which there is a constant attempt to discover what is visually appealing and exotic. Such regimes of visual representation have re-emerged as strategies for representing Ireland today. In this respect, there is an unconscious process by which those organisations involved in heritage representations, like Bord Failte, have come to internalise these depictions of Ireland. Following this, then, images of our heritage have, according to O'Connor,[2] tended to link in to pre-existing images of Ireland forged elsewhere.

Like the traditional museum, the heritage centre must employ a variety of techniques for presenting the past, such as photographs, audio-visual displays, holograms etc. Objects and places cannot speak for themselves – they have to be mediated in some way. In the traditional museum, objects were given meaning through written captions and the order of their display. In the heritage centre, different media and

2   Barbara O'Connor, "Myths and mirrors: tourist images and national identity", in Barbara O'Connor and Michael Cronin (eds), *Tourism in Ireland: a critical analysis,* Cork: Cork University Press, 1993

processes are used to convey the past. The visualisation process, with its use of images and simulation, helps the centre to fulfil its function of translating information for a wide and varied audience while at the same time providing an entertaining experience.

Heritage as tourist activity

These current modes of representing the past are determined by touristic practices. For John Urry,[3] touristic practice involves the notion of *departure*, of a limited breaking with the established routines and practices of everyday life and allowing one's senses to engage with a set of stimuli that contrast with everyday life and the mundane. This notion of departure, then, becomes a useful tool in understanding tourism, but also the heritage industry. As people desire to escape from their everyday existence for a short period each year, they seek the exotic. It is because they endeavour to satisfy this desire of the tourist that it is vital for the heritage industry to reproduce the exotic.

The rise in popularity of heritage has accompanied the fall in interest in the seaside resort as the main object of the tourist gaze. Again this change was brought about by various social developments. In the first place, a country's heritage could be used to counteract the growing internationalisation of tourism, with its preference for seaside resorts in the sun. As well as this, heritage began to be perceived as a resource to promote economic development in the locality. Local heritage was used in the race between regions to exploit a local sense of place and attract the global tourist. In the third place, the emerging *service class* moved away from the traditional object of the tourist gaze. This class across the globe, according to Urry,[4] are made up of those who do not own land or capital to any substantial degree; who are located

3 John Urry, *The tourist gaze*, London: Sage, 1990
4 *ibid*, pp 88-9

within a set of interlocking social institutions which col-
lectively service capital; who enjoy superior work and market
situations, have well-defined careers and the required
educational credentials. These classes consume cultural products in a conspicuous way, as part of a claim for distinction:
they are no longer satisfied by the traditional visit to the
seaside. And, finally, heritage objects allow the tourism
industry to provide for the needs of nostalgia which activate
a certain *fondness* for the past.[5] Heritage therefore gradually
became a crucial component in the Irish tourism industry in
that it came to be envisaged as the new desired object of the
tourist gaze, and so became the tourism industry's most
important product. It was responding to global trends, by
offering distinctive and extraordinary objects to gaze upon.

The main tourism priority in this country for the 1990s
has been to target our key strengths which Bord Failte lists
as: superb scenic landscapes; a quiet island with a relaxed
pace of life; a distinctive heritage and culture; an absence of
mass tourism; a friendly, welcoming, convivial people; and a
green unspoilt environment. The various agencies involved
in the tourism industry have planned to exploit various
aspects of Irish life, package these as our tourist product and
promote them in international markets, and in this process
provide the types of experience which tourists desire. In
answering the worldwide demand for heritage, Bord Failte
believes that Ireland will satisfy visitors' demand for the
distinctive and extraordinary gaze whilst on holiday, through
the enhancement of our heritage attractions

Heritage, then, is dictated mainly by the needs of tourism.
One of the main priorities for the heritage industry is proper
interpretation of our past. In its strategy for interpretation,
the emphasis is put on constructing an overall and unique
product. This product is like a book containing chapters which
relate the story of Ireland's heritage for the foreign and

---

5 David Lowentahl, *The past in a foreign country*, Cambridge:
Cambridge University Press, 1985

45

domestic visitor. It consists of a framework of themes and storylines to be developed at different heritage sites, around which Ireland's culture and heritage can be interpreted to visitors. The interpretive gateways into Ireland's heritage aim to heighten visitors' experience, to create a strong brand image of Ireland as a quality heritage destination with unique, distinctive attractions – all geared towards attracting more visitors and more visitor spending.

Heritage as leisure

The heritage experience is increasingly seen in terms of providing pleasure, as much as conveying knowledge and information on Ireland's past. In this regard, the predominance of the visual over the verbal in heritage centre displays illustrates how the heritage and tourism industries are striving to meet the needs of tourists. There seems to be an urgent wish to achieve an immediate confrontation with the past on the part of visitors, and this is provided for in the heritage centres' employment of the visual image in its displays. The visualisation process enables the tourism and heritage industries to package aspects of a culture, translating information for a wide and varied audience, while at the same time providing a pleasurable experience.

Thus heritage, as a product of tourism, is meant to provide pleasure. Pervasive throughout the heritage industry, I believe, is a pursuit of pleasure. Tourism, as we noted, was ultimately a quest for pleasurable experience, away from regulated and organised work, with the places gazed upon being chosen because they promised intense pleasures. With the growing interest in heritage as an increasingly popular object of the tourist gaze, the desires were the same. Visitors wanted immediate confrontation with the past, immediate pleasure. Thus, what has happened is that pleasure has simply come to be anticipated and experienced in different ways than before. Towns and cities began to be re-constructed as centres of consumption in themselves and, most importantly, as sites of pleasure. In the heritage centre, this need

46

for pleasure was provided for through the creation of inherently romantic images from the past. This allowed for a more entertaining way of looking into, and even participating in, the past; the pursuit of knowledge becomes attractive for its promised pleasurable effects, rather than because of any great interest in the past. The visual experience offered by heritage attractions could bring sites to life with actors and animators, with stories being told through pictures. The modes of representation, then, altered according to the changing needs of society and the changing perceptions of those embarking on travel.

Mere spectators to their own past

Heritage is then a mode of representing the world, its histories and its cultures in ways different to the representation of the world in the traditional museum. The differing regimes of representation themselves point to social changes that have occurred since the nineteenth century. The underlying function performed by the two institutions differs greatly. The traditional museum's collection for scholarly use contrasts with the heritage centre's emphasis on providing visitors with an immediate confrontation with the past. The methods of representing the past in the traditional museum – the accumulation of rare and priceless artifacts, and the subsequent ordering, displaying and labelling of these – were seen as the most effective way towards the instruction and edification of the general public. In the heritage centre, the modes of representing the past strive towards providing the visitor with an enjoyable experience. As Malcolm Crick[6] observed, for most people tourism involves more hedonism and conspicuous consumption than learning or understanding.

However, these new modes of representation of the past

---

6 Malcolm Crick, "Representations of international tourism in the social sciences", *Annual Review of Anthropology*, vol 18 (1989), p 328

do not sustain a sense of critical distance and of historical time. Because of this, important issues are not made explicit. For example, heritage creates a deep division between professionals involved in heritage representations and both the visitors and the local populations surrounding the heritage sites. This was already stressed in the study of museums of the nineteenth century, wherein methods of representation were adopted which naturally negated criticism or questioning, and which helped maintain the status quo. These museums, although promoted as being for the people, were most definitely not by the people in that they kept the general public from any involvement in museum operation or policy. In the heritage centres, this has not changed. Although the modes of representing the past have altered, selection processes still remain implicit. The visitor must continue to place trust in the professional bodies responsible for heritage representations. The heritage centre's curator still maintains control over what is put on show. The tourist gaze is not left to chance. Heritage attractions are constructed by heritage professionals only.

The role of professionals in the area of heritage representation is a matter of even greater concern for the local populations surrounding heritage sites. In this case, the resident's own local history is being displayed with usually no input from the locals themselves. Those people then, who are most directly affected by the presence of a heritage attraction through the impact of visitor numbers and, most importantly, whose own heritage is being used to attract these visitors, have in effect the least amount of involvement in representation. The resident population becomes in a sense mere spectators of their own past.

... the local becoming global ...

CHAPTER 4

Riverdance

BARBARA O'CONNOR

This year, 1997 marks the centenary of the first Gaelic League céilí, held in Bloomsbury Hall, London, and which represented one of the early efforts to involve dance in the project of cultural nationalism. From the turn of the century, Irish dance has been shaped in keeping with the cultural and political requirements of the emerging nation-state. The process involved the selection of certain dance repertoires and styles and the omission of others to create an *authentic* national canon, that is to say a generally accepted style of dancing.[1] And then, almost one hundred years later, along came *Riverdance*, marking yet another transformation in Irish dance. This time, however, the dance was not part of a project of cultural nationalism but was shaped in keeping with the requirements of production for an international audience and a global market. And it, too, was highly successful.

Global dancing

More than any other Irish cultural production in the last decade, *Riverdance* has achieved success not only in box office terms, in London, New York, and Sydney, but also in terms

---

1 see, for example, Helen Brennan, "Reinventing tradition: the boundaries of Irish dance", in *History Ireland*, Summer 1994

of media publicity and critical acclaim. It has already been woven into popular culture. Michael Flatley and Jean Butler, the original lead dancers, have achieved celebrity status and have appeared on the top-rating television chat shows as well as in the social columns of the national and international press. The show has been the subject of television documentary (*Downstream from Riverdance*) on the adoption of Irish step dancing by Northern Irish Protestants and an inspiration for television drama (*Dance, Lexi, Dance*). Because of its unprecedented success, *Riverdance* has in the popular imagination come to be regarded as synonymous with *Irish* dance.

In critical terms, *Riverdance* has generally been hailed as a high point of cultural achievement of which Irish people can be proud. It is regarded as the marker of the leap from a repressed and puritanical culture, the province of fanatics and *Gaeilgeoirí* where dancing was regimented and boring, to a neo-liberal one in which dance was transformed into something which was exciting, sexy and exuberant. Indeed, the main critical discourse, almost exclusively journalistic to date and expressed by columnists such as Fintan O'Toole,[2] has presented *Riverdance* as the confident expression of a culture which can embrace traditional art forms by breaking them apart and reconstructing them in an imaginative and innovative way. Irish cultural expression in this scenario is seen to have now reached the point where it has overcome a sense of post-colonial inferiority and can take its place confidently on the world stage. *Riverdance* is perceived as the liberating moment of Irish dance. However, another form of critical discourse has been largely absent from the discussion of *Riverdance*, a discourse which sees culture as becoming increasingly commodified. Within this scenario, local cultural expression is appropriated by cultural entrepreneurs for the global marketplace and in the process loses its authenticiy and value.

---

2 Fintan O'Toole, "Unsuitables from a distance: the politics of Riverdance', in *Ex-Isle of Erin: images of a global Ireland*, Dublin: New Island Books, 1997

From local to global

The success of *Riverdance* raises a number of questions concerning the relationship between the local and the global levels of cultural expression and production. A particular brand of *Irishness* is sucessfully projected onto the world scene through *Riverdance*. But Irish dance is transformed by going global.

Irish dance is a hybrid form. It is true to say that it has been influenced from abroad from at least the eighteenth century. The origins of set dancing in the *quadrilles* and *cotillons* introduced from Britain and France provide just one example. In addition, some forms of dance attain dominance at a particular time, such as céilí dancing. The popularisation of céilí dancing marginalised, though did not eliminate, older styles of rural solo step dancing and set dancing which continued to be part of a vibrant dance tradition in the west of Ireland. The irony is that while set dancing was frowned upon because of its "foreignness", it was the traditional form of dance for many parts of the country. Dancing then, like any other cultural form, is continuously evolving, and particular styles of dance both reflect and reproduce the social and cultural environment in which dance events occur.

I would like to suggest, somewhat schematically, that the historical trajectory of Irish step dancing from the beginning of this century has followed the expansion of its geographical range, from local, through national, to global contexts. Each of these moments shaped the forms of dance in distinctive ways; certain repertoires and styles were encouraged or even demanded by different kinds of institutional and performance context. The local rural context was one in which dancing formed an integral part of local entertainment and was performed most often in domestic settings on both everyday occasions such as "rambling" and in more special ritual festivities such as weddings, harvest, St Stephen's Day. The national context was organised almost exclusively around competition dancing (*feiseanna*) in which cultural organisations like the Gaelic League and later Coimisiún na Rinncí

Gaelacha played a key role in the standardisation of dance styles. They achieved a virtual monopoly of Irish dance regulation and practice, and were responsible for the introduction of the styles which we now regard as rigid and restrictive. This standard national style became the dominant representation of Irish dance, providing us with the visual motifs of young girls in elaborate dancing costumes and ringlets, stepping it out in a stiff and earnest manner. This period has been followed by the *international* style exemplified by *Riverdance* in which the performance has become a commodified form for distribution in the global marketplace.

Spectacle and medley

The evolutionary path from local, through national, to international dance performance contexts, and back, has been characterised by an increasing emphasis on visual impact and on spectacle. Visual interest is achieved through variety, which usually entails a combination of performance elements. *Riverdance* is a full theatrical production including music, song, and dance performances as well as a narrative thread. This kind of eclecticism in Irish dance did not begin with *Riverdance*, and its origins might well be traced to 1970 when the World Championships in Irish Dancing included for the first time competitions for choreography. As Brendan Breathnach observed, "footwork for its own sake was giving way to movement and colour which, with music, decor and dress, combined in a dance drama to present and illustrate some motif of Irish significance: an historical event, a social custom or story",[3] And it is worth noting that, at the time of writing, the dance drama was the most popular event at the championships. Neither is it a coincidence, in my view, that the World Championships themselves had been initiated just one year earlier in 1969, establishing the link between international influences and more spectacular dance forms.

3   Breandan Breathnach, *Dancing in Ireland*, Miltown Malbay, Co Clare: Dal gCais Publications, 1983

Riverdance started life as pure spectacle in its initial incarnation as the seven minute interval performance for the Eurovision song contest of 1994. Eurovision is one of a few annual live television events with a massive viewership (allegedly, in this instance, three hundred millions). It was created with spectacle and an international audience in mind. The show's producer, Moya Doherty, set out to achieve maximum visual impact in her initial conceptualisation of the project. In a memo which included, inter alia, the shape of the piece she envisaged, she wrote:

> We begin with a lonely band of musicians on a big empty stage, enter the pageantry up the centre of the audi-torium, a hundred marching Bodhran players .... all this with a chorus of Irish voices ... From a point of darkness ... enter row upon row of hard-shoe Irish dancers and they pound their way downstage towards audience and camera. They stream apart to the dramatic entrance of the star dancers who perform their energetic routine. Gradually the tempo increases, bringing all the ingredients together in an exhilarating climax.[4]

The winning formula of the Eurovision performance was followed through into *Riverdance* the show, in terms of the scale of production. The provision of a wide stage meant that the dancers had much more space at their disposal than they would have had in other more traditional performance situations. Compare it for instance to local performance spaces in domestic kitchens where the confined nature of the space placed emphasis on the vertical floor tapping and where dancing in place came to be valorised. In competitive step dancing the stage allowed for, indeed demanded, more horizontal movements as the adjudicators award marks for the use made of the stage space by competitors. The dance

---

4   quoted in Sam Smyth, *Riverdance: the story,* London: Andre Deutsch, 1996, p 24

style demanded by *Riverdance* is one which requires filling the stage with maximum visual impact. And within the global performance context, the dance styles and repertoires must also traverse a fine line between familiarity and exoticism. The exoticism is provided by what is regarded as distinctly Irish and different, and the familiarity by dance styles and techniques which have already become internationally disseminated by the mass media of film and television, especially those of Hollywood musicals. The horizontal movements of Michael Flatley across the stage, with his frequent use of high leaps and jumps, are dramatic, extravagant, expansive. One might like to think that he is mimicking the rural solo and duet dances of the eighteenth century which, according to the available evidence, were also characterised by leaps, jumps and high-stepping. It seems more likely, though, that his stepping style is influenced by those which have already been visually popularised, such as tap, Flamenco, modern dance, and ballet.

In choreographic terms, then, *Riverdance* borrows much from the style of popular American stage and film musicals of the 1920s to 1950s, and it seems only fitting that the venue for the New York version of the show was Radio City Music Hall in Manhattan, the home of the American theatrical dance and musical productions. This is evident in the sheer size of the cast. The serried rows of dancers fill the stage, providing what has been termed a "feeling of abundance". As Robert Ballagh comments, "*Riverdance* wouldn't work with six dancers no matter how brilliant they were. What makes it work is the scale of the spectacle".[5] Not only is the large number of dancers providing visual interest, but it also generates the emotional charge of the mass impact of dancing feet.

The elements of traditional Irish dance which remain least changed are the vertical movements of dancers. These include the rigid upper body stance, the straight arm position, and

---

5   quoted in Smyth, *op cit*, p 107

aspects of the stepping technique. But these traditional postures and steps are being continually contrasted with the freer horizontal movements of other types of modern dance. The dancers' use of space, therefore, highlights the contrast between the more expansive horizontal movements (associated with non-Irish dance) and the vertical movements (associated with Irish dance). The exotic nature of *Riverdance* is partly explained by this contrast in styles.

Of crucial importance in the creation of visual interest and excitement is costume. Here again we can see a gradual process of increased visualisation ranging from the ordinary clothes worn by traditional rural set dancers to the introduction of special costumes for competitive step dancers from the early part of the century, with an ever increasing emphasis on decoration and embellishment (particularly in girls' costumes). Breathnach's remarks are instructive in relation to the meanings of the dress codes of competitive step-dancing: "the costumes display an Irishness which eludes any association with a particular locality or period".[6] Not only do the costumes in question signify an abstract and anodyne Irishness, but they also have the effect of hiding the body by attracting the eye to the interlaced Celtic motifs, tara brooches, lace collars and medals on the dancer's costumes.

Riverdance moved right away from this style. The costumes of the principal dancers are very definitely showbiz: materials which shine, encrusted and glitzy; note the off the shoulder dresses for Jean Butler and the satin open-necked shirts for Michael Flatley with decorated cumberbund. Yet the female dance troupe's costumes are stark in their simplicity. The materials are also "soft, flowing, revealing the contours of the body", according to the costume designer Jen Kelly. Both the use of soft materials and the simplicity of design emphasise the contours of the body. The same simplicity is a feature of the male dancers' costumes; black trousers and shirts in some sequences, or short-sleeved tee-shirts which

---

6 Breathnach, *op cit*, p 49

reveal their biceps. While it is worth noting that the costumes tend to sexualise both male and female bodies by subjecting them to the gaze, the female bodies are also additionally sexualised by the use of the age old convention of shorter than regulation dresses which expose their legs.

One of the most striking characteristics of *Riverdance* is the fast pace of the dance which generates a sense of excitement and energy, and points to the virtuosity and skill of individual performances. There is of course a dialectical relationship between the speed of the music and the dance. It is worth noting that Irish traditional music (apart from slow airs) was called Irish *dance* music and was traditionally played for the dancers, so that the tempo of the dance were in accord. During the competitive era, there was a gradual separating out of dance music from dance because of two developments. The introduction of a highly ornate dance style meant that the music for dancers was played much more slowly than the normal tempo and, with the introduction of mass media, musicians became performers in their own right. *Riverdance* seems to have taken the relationship full circle, from a situation in which musicians played for dancers, through an era in which musicians played primarily as individual and virtuoso performers, to a situation where musicians and dancers are again connecting but where the dancing is at a much faster pace than in either local or national competitive performance situations.

The orchestra's presence on stage provides the visual link between dancers and musicians. The musical and dance performances are also intertwined as in the scene (in the New York show) where the fiddle player, Eileen Ivers, walks on stage and plays a tune on a bright blue fiddle, or in the *Trading Taps* scene in the same show where both Ivers and the jazz musician play for, and to, the rival gangs in the street scene. The intertwining is also highlighted in sequences where initial solo or troupe stepping without musical accompaniment is followed by the musical instrumentals echoing the rhythm of the dancers' feet and vice versa.

The speed of the dance performance is conveyed to the

audience primarily through sound and a number of techniques are used to highlight it. One is the frequent use of routines which start out with a slow beat and, gradually, the tempo increases to arrive at a high speed crescendo or climax. The synchronised and insistent sound of the full troupe battering out a hard shoe dance is undoubtedly one of the highlights of the show. Because of the importance of rhythmic sound, the emphasis has to be on footwork which maximises sound and which consequently allows for little variation in stepping technique or style. So at the same time as the dancers (Flatley and the male dancers especially) use an eclectic mix of dance styles, their "Irish" style does not utilise the possible range of steps and repertoire that are common in less spectacular and more traditional performance settings.

But the *pièce de resistance* in the fusion of music and dance, of sight and sound, springs from the use of radio microphones in the insteps of the principal dancers' shoes. The rationale for this dramatic amplification effect is explained by the sound designer Michael O'Gorman: "a natural sound works best with traditional music, that it needs to sound as if the musicians are playing right in front of you without amplification, unlike a rock concert where the reverb is part of the occasion". This *technologising* of the body effectively turns the body itself into a musical instrument.

Globalisation and hybridity

In this chapter, I have suggested that the dominant performance styles, and the meanings and pleasures of dance, have changed and evolved in response to the changes from a local, to a national, to an international context. Within this framework, *Riverdance* can be seen as a marker of a transformation of Irish dance into a form which is suitable for global consumption: a form which places maximum emphasis on spectacle and which reflects the primacy of the visualisation of cultural production in contemporary society.

The projection of an Irish cultural product, such as *River-*

dance, onto the world scene required that it underwent a major transformation. It had of course to take the form of a commodity. It was not simply a matter of Irish dancing losing its popular roots and being commercialised. Irish dancing could assume the status of a global commodity only by mixing with other cultural forms, by becoming a *hybrid*. But the melange of cultural forms is not left to chance:

> ... we can construct a continuum of hybridities: on one end, an assimilationist hybridity that leans over towards the centre, adopts and mimics the hegemony, and, at the other end, a destabilizing hybridity that blurs the canon, reverse the current, subverts the centre. Hybridities, then, may be differentiated according to the components of the melange.[7]

The previous analysis suggests that the Irishness of *Riverdance* does not blur, reverse or subvert the centre by becoming hybrid. It has become a global commodity by adopting the cultural frame of the centre.

But such a hybrid form does not leave untouched the cultural forms on which it feeds. *Riverdance* has generally been hailed as one of the signs of a national culture reaching maturity: sufficiently self-confident about our traditional culture to successfully take our place on the global cultural stage. The trajectory from the local to the global has had the effect, in some respects at least, of closing down possibilities for Irish dance. The globalisation of cultural production places increasing emphasis on visualisation and spectacle. Those aspects of Irish dance which do not easily fit this framework are evacuated, while those aspects which enhance the creation of spectacle are pursued.

7 Jan Nederveen Pieterse, "Globalization as hybridization", in Mike Featherstone, Scott Lash and Roland Robertson (eds), *Global modernities,* London: Sage, 1995, pp 56-7

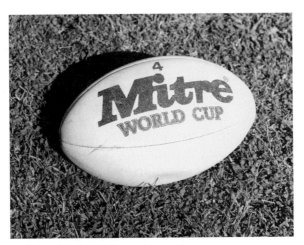

... the new playmaker ...

CHAPTER 5

Dependent Rugby

EAMONN SLATER

O n Saturday 15 February 1997, England beat Ireland by a record number of points. The old enemy had won again! But this time the score indicated not only the dominance of the English team over the Irish on the playing field, but also the growing dominance of British capital over Irish capital in the organisational structure of the game. In the last two years, the game of rugby has undergone a dramatic sea-change in its development worldwide. The sport has become professional and, as a consequence, it now falls under the sway of a new set of laws and regulations, those of the market. This ushers in a new era in the evolution of the game of rugby as a sport. The most dramatic feature of the new modern game is that the best players are now being paid to play. But the appearance of professional players within the game is not the beginning of the process of making it a marketable commodity, but the final stage of the *takeover*.

An Alamo of amateurism

Rugby was ideally suited for such a takeover. As the last great amateur sport in the world, it has had a large following worldwide, especially in those parts of the globe that were

The author would like to thank Declan Smith for his comments on an earlier version of this article.

successfully colonised by the British. As its origins indicate, rugby was an elite sport, played by a colonising elite, middle class and upper, and played in the time honoured tradition of playing for *the fun of it*. Played by gentlemen against gentlemen, and played for gentlemanly pride only. Much was excluded from this world of gentlemenly sport; the ugly world of business and finance was kept at a distance. And when money did attempt to enter the hallowed grounds of the game, a schism was created to deal with this attempted heretical reformation. Those heretics who wanted to redefine the essential principles of amateurism were unceremoniously dumped and condemned to spend the rest of their playing careers within the confines of Rugby League, a game created specifically to be played for money, and accordingly played by *non-gentlemen*. The Rugby League schism from Rugby Union was finally ratified by the enactment of a ban, which prevented those who had fallen from grace and taken up Rugby League from rejoining the ranks of the chosen few, the middle-class amateurs of Rugby Union. The personal cost of this financial avarice was eternal banishment. But these ancient walls of amateurism, which had so long protected the game, have been finally breached by capital, by a radically new form of *spectacular* capital. This form of capital is unique in its ability to see and be seen at the same time: it is media capital.

Rugby as a visual commodity

I want to show how the modern game of rugby in Ireland has become a marketable commodity and to assess the consequences of this for the structure of the game. To fully understand the takeover, we need to examine the concept of media capital. The consequence of the penetration of media capital into the sport is not only the emerging growing dominance of money in the structuring of the modern game but also the manner in which the game is becoming more of a spectacle[1] rather than a mere sporting activity. In short, the

1   Guy Debord, *The society of the spectacle*, New York: Zone Books, 1995

64

price to be paid for commercialising the game is that the game has to become a spectacle within the media industries. Media capital operates in the world of the media industries, especially television broadcasting.[2] Events are broadcast because they can be sold as a commodity to the viewing public directly or to other media companies throughout the globe. As a result, local events like the England/Ireland match at Lansdowne Road can become global events when they are transformed into visual commodities in transnational broadcasting. The public can pay to see such games in several ways. Traditionally, most people pay through their licensing fee. However, there is a growing trend of paying to see a particular match through cable TV. Media capital generates money because it is able to monitor the match and broadcast it to the viewing public. The commodity which media capital creates and sells is a mediated representation of an event. With technical devices like action replay, it produces particular views of the match from exotic angles and provides an interpretation of what is happening through the commentary. But media capital can operate at a level other than its ability to show and comment: for it can also be seen. In this case, media capital reconstructs the physical environment in which the game is being played in order to send out messages to the public. Here, advertisements are displayed within the range of the TV cameras. Therefore, the seeing and being seen forms of media capital depend on each other. Let us attempt to assess the effect of media capital on the game of rugby and how it has penetrated into this *Alamo* of amateurism.

Media capital as the new play-maker

In making the game a spectacle, media capital has indirectly affected how the game is being played. The laws of the game have been recently rewritten in order to respond to demands

---

2 John B. Thompson, *Ideology and modern culture,* Cambridge: Polity Press, 1990

to make the game more visibly attractive and more comprehensible to a non-expert viewing public. These new laws attempt to create a more dramatic event, by encouraging more of the running game and thereby increasing the amount of exciting moments produced within a match. The pinnacle of the game is the scoring of a try and the number of points awarded for a try has accordingly been increased from three to five points in an attempt to encourage teams to adopt try-scoring strategies in their game plans. Not surprisingly, any blockage to the desired flowing movement of the running game is now severely dealt with by the laws; this is illustrated by the dramatic increase in awarding the penalty-try in recent years. Ironically, one consequence of these changes in the laws of the game is to make Rugby Union similar to Rugby League in its structure. With all of this newly created excitement on the field of play, media capital could not resist the temptation of getting as close as possible to the action.

We can get some idea of the degree of this penetration by recalling the appearance of the ground at Lansdowne Road on the dismal day of Ireland's defeat by England. The pitch itself is ringed by low advertisement boards, displaying logos and messages from Irish and international companies. This ring of commodity symbols is *sacred*! Sacred to the almighty seeing eye of the television camera. No prolonged activity (except the game itself) can take place in front of these sacred boards. Team officials, security officials, and especially photographers must either remain behind the advertisement hoardings or constantly move along, least they interfere with the visibility of the sponsor's message to the world. One of the tasks of the security officials is to make sure no one blocks the view to these boards. On this sad occasion for Irish rugby, high tech advertisement made its appearance in Lansdowne Road for the first time. Tucked away in a corner, but not out of range of the TV cameras, a rotating advertisement board changed its message to the world every few minutes. In fact the actual changeover of these messages themselves had a tendency to distract one's attention from the game, and one might suggest that this distraction tended to occur more among the Irish supporters than the English fans. This new electronic board can draw attention to itself and increase the amount of messages it delivers from the same spatial confines of the more conventional boards. But the advertisement invasion does not stop here; it actually has spilled onto the playing surface of the pitch in a number of ways.

On the goal posts and on the playing area behind these posts, advertisements appear on the physical surfaces. These displays are constructed to be exclusively seen through the lens of the TV camera. Behind the goal posts, the message is painted onto the grass in such a way and at such an angle than it can barely be deciphered from the terraces; but it can be easily seen on the TV screen. With regard to the goal posts, the actual style of the padding has been changed in order to facilitate the visibility of its printed message, i.e. from being rounded and curved to being rectangular and square shaped. These displays are stationary, but there are others which move with the play on the pitch because they are attached to the players themselves. The logo and even the name of global sportswear companies are identifiable on the playing strip and the boots of the players. The players of the game have become beacons for global companies. But, even more importantly than this visible display of commodity endorsement on the players' sportswear, the players and their play are now providing a visually exotic performance to a background which is visually dominated by media capital. However, the background of media capital is not just a passive backdrop to the more important foreground of the play; it is actually determining the whole structure of the game both on and off the field. The new professional players themselves have become dependent on media capital for their wages.

Paying Irish players to play British rugby

Two years ago, the green light was given to the rugby clubs by their respective rugby football unions to pay players. The most interesting aspect of this financial deal was not how much the players were going to earn but where the money was to come from? The funds were to come from the Rugby Football Union's contract with the TV companies. This led to a number of protracted disputes, initially between the TV companies and the Unions (and between the Unions themselves) and later between the Unions and their rugby clubs. But there has been a huge difference between the ways in which the English and Irish Unions attempted to resolve the dispute with their clubs. This difference highlights the contrast between Ireland and England with regard to the uneven development of capital penetration into the game of rugby.

In England, because the TV deal was not agreed to until late in the day, the clubs were left to speculate on how much they were going to get from the TV funds. They had to begin the process of professionalisation without confirmation of the exact funds to be released by the Rugby Union or get left behind in the dash for glory (or survival). Most of these clubs presumed they would each be getting a one million pound handout. This turned out to be wrong and clubs had to make do with less than half that figure. By that time, most top-class rugby players had been persuaded to switch from part-time to full-time positions, which meant giving up their day jobs. The problem now emerges that the vast majority of English and Welsh clubs can afford to pay neither the transfer fees nor wages of these modern professional players. The question is now being asked: is the whole process sustainable? And since the TV funds are not maintaining the necessary cash flow, alternative sources are being sought. One big hope was that professional club rugby, because of its new exciting media image, would draw bigger attendance crowds. In Britain, attendances have edged up, yet the average is still incredibly low when compared to soccer. In soccer, it has been estimated that a club needs to get gate receipts which can cover at least fifty per cent of the wage bill. The gate receipts of some second division rugby clubs in Britain only amount to six per cent of their expenditure. One way of overcoming the low attendance figures has been to charge more to those who do attend. Admission prices to club games have in certain cases gone up by a large percentage, rising to as much as fifteen pounds seated and ten pounds standing (*The Observer*, 16 February 1997).

With regard to Ireland, the most dramatic example of increasing costs of attending rugby games has occurred at the international level. From next year the price of the exclusive three-year stand ticket package will be £1,250. With a maximum of five games per season, this means that each ticket costs over eighty-three pounds, compared to thirty pounds stand ticket for the English game already referred to (*Irish Independent*, 14 February 1997). Quite clearly, this offer is designed to interest the corporate sector rather than the ordinary rugby supporter.

This highlights the trend of rugby becoming a spectacle. The corporate bodies are buying into the spectacle as a way of entertaining their clients, and the chosen few can enjoy the privilege of being seen on the prestigious occasion. Also, a large majority of Irish clubs sell a proportion of their international ticket allocation to their respective corporate sponsors as a way of raising working capital.

Irish clubs cannot afford to professionalise to the same extent as the British clubs. There is not sufficient support to sustain a professional squad of players within each club, either from local attendance or from the TV audience. The domestic market is too small to launch this new product as an exclusively Irish commodity. As a consequence, Irish rugby can only survive as an entity by becoming a global commodity. And it becomes a global product when the game is played against international opposition. In this light, international competition creates the material base for the emergence of Irish rugby as a global product in the world of the media. Therefore, the best of Irish players who want to play professional rugby have to play it outside Ireland, and generally in Britain. Of the fifteen Irish players on the pitch at Lansdowne, nine of them were employed by English clubs. Here, we have a modern example of an old economic dependent relationship of Ireland on Britain. Because of the under-developed nature of the Irish economy, Ireland had to export its raw materials to Britain to be transformed into industrial commodities. Ireland's economic survival became dependent on the sale of those raw materials to the British market.[3] Irish rugby will likewise become increasingly dependent of the whims of British rugby and its new *play-maker* of media capital. The old foe will dominate us not only on the field of play as it did on 15 February 1997, but also in the new global market of media capital.

---

3   Denis O'Hearn, "The Irish case of dependency: an exception to the exceptions", *American Sociological Review*, vol 54 (1989)

SIGNS OF THE TIME

CHAPTER 6

A Religious Frenzy?

TOM INGLIS

Sometimes it seems that sport and popular music are replacing religion in Ireland, at least in terms of popular devotion. Think of the country coming to a standstill during the Ireland-Italy soccer match in the 1994 World Cup. The only other event to achieve such national adulation was the visit of Pope John Paul II in 1979. The Pope is undoubtedly a holy man. But think of the hundreds of thousands of young Irish people who cram into rock concerts and scream and clamour for their idols. And whose images do young people have before them on their bedroom walls? Are these the false gods about which we have been warned? If we are looking for one clear sign of how holy Catholic Ireland has been overtaken by modernity and secularisation, is this media-driven, popular consumer culture not it?

Perhaps the fundamental Islamic view of the West is right. Maybe we are nothing more than fat Roman cats heading to the Coliseum; abandoning the ethical good life while sinking into a pagan sea of hedonistic pleasure. Or maybe it is not as simple as this. It could be that what we regard as sacred; what binds people together into different identities and communities is changing rapidly. It could be that instead of religion being taken over by popular culture, the nature of what is religious and sacred is changing.

Sacredness

Sacredness refers to persons, places or things which are set apart as different, out of the ordinary, i.e. supernatural. The French sociologist Emile Durkheim[1] was adamant that this notion of sacredness was central to understanding religious life. While anything could be regarded as sacred, any disregard or mistreatment of the sacred object was an act of profanity. Religion then, for Durkheim, relates to collective rituals and beliefs concerning sacred things which unite people into a community. In a way, anything, any collective representation which brings and binds people together is religious and anything which detracts from this, which is private and individual, is profane. The crucifix is a traditional example of a sacred icon; a Manchester United scarf is a more contemporary one.

Now maybe putting christians and Manchester United soccer supporters into the same boat is to push the argument out too far. One could argue that while soccer players and pop groups generate passionate commitment, loyalty and excitement among their followers, there is nothing godly, supernatural or even magical about them. More important from Durkheim's point of view, while they may both have collective rituals (matches and concerts), there are no orthodox beliefs which unite their followers into anything like a Church – although I did once come across the Church of Man United, but it was in the middle of America.

Maybe what is happening is that in an era of relativity and pluralism, religious life has become low on orthodox belief and strong on collective ritual. Rituals help create what Durkheim called "collective effervesence" which is central to the sacrifice of the self and the generation of identity and belonging. The ritual gathering to witness and participate in the same activities, the generation of excitement, brings people out of themselves and into the group. What is happen-

---

1 Emile Durkheim, *The elementary forms of the religious life*, London: Allen and Unwin, 1915

ing in Ireland is that, with some exceptions, religious rituals have become empty formulae which, particularly for the younger generation, no longer generate the same excitement and passion as soccer matches and rock concerts.

Sociologists have long recognised that religious experience or fervour is an important dimension of religious life. In Catholic Ireland, popular religious devotions such as novenas, missions, pattern days and pilgrimages still produce intense religious experiences. But over the past hundred years, it seems to have been part of Catholic Church policy to push these devotions to the periphery. The institutional church has always been disdainful of unregulated religious excitement, even at the level of charismatic prayer group meetings. It may be one thing to gain a sense of the supernatural through religious experiences, but religious fervour can easily become a frenzy and people can loose the run of themselves completely. For the Catholic Church this poses the problem that the people involved may not end up back in church. As a priest once told me when I noted the Church's disdain for religious experience: "what begins in mist often ends in schism". But the generation of collective effervesence is central to religious life and if the institutional Church will not provide it, it will emerge elsewhere. One of the main reasons behind the moving statues phenomenon in the summer of 1985 was not so much the decline in the economy as the decline in popular devotions and religious fervour within the Church.

Despite the salutation of Pope John Paul to the young people of Ireland, increasing numbers of them are turning to sport and popular music for collective rituals which engender not just excitement, but an oceanic experience of otherness. It used to be that religious imagery in churches, the robes, the incense, the hymns and incantations generated a spiritual feeling which, in turn, facilitated a surrender to the group. Now it is sport and popular music, often aided by drugs, which generate those oceanic feelings of selflessness and otherness which create and maintain a sense of belonging. Besides, sport and popular music are unfettered by ethics and archaic language. There is something about such events which young people can experience and share with each other.

One of the reasons why religion is failing in Ireland as it has done in other Western societies is because, unlike sport and popular music, it is not a media event. With the odd exception, such as Pope John Paul II, there is little or no public relations, stage management and collaboration with the media to stage religious events. This is because the Church has not adapted to the media. It still treats the media like a disobedient child. One can sympathise with the Church. It is damned if it does collaborate with the media and it is damned if it does not. See what has happened to Christmas. The one religious event which still does generate a huge sense of attachment, identity and excitement has been hijacked by commercial forces sponsored by the media.

The media and modern frenzy

Without the media hype beforehand, some sports events would generate no more excitement than a race between two snails. It is the active collaboration between sports promoters, commercial bodies, technology and the media which creates the excitement. Companies sponsor the event, specific teams and contestants. The media build up the excitement and provide the coverage. For example, in the weeks in advance of an event like the World Cup, the public is fed a series of reports, features, inside stories, anecdotes, analyses and prognostications which create an anticipation of excitement. By the time the big match begins, the streets have been emptied, the pubs filled with supporters, many of whom have worked themselves into a mild, well-mannered ecstatic frenzy. Friends, family members and bare acquaintances come together to surrender themselves to what is happening on the altar of sport. Through the use of a huge number of cameras, slow-action replays, detailed commentaries and analyses, every aspect of the play can be drooled over in pornographic-like detail. It is the engagement in this collective ritual which creates and maintains a sense of common cause and belief;

of surrendering oneself to an interest and passion which envelops one's whole being.

But it would be wrong to think that big matches and pop concerts are just regular once-off events which have no lasting meaning or influence. There is a way of being which centres around following a particular team or pop group. One does not become a dedicated follower easily. There is a knowledge to be acquired, paraphernalia to be bought, terminology and references to be mastered, pilgrimages to be made and experiences to be had. For the devotees there is in-depth knowledge of the stars, their performances, scores, habits, likes and dislikes. Stars of sport and popular music are like saints; they have their particular attractions and attributes, and followers have their particular favourites.

I happened to be in a hotel in Dundalk on Saturday, 11 May 1996; the day Manchester United won the English FA League and Cup double. It could have been any other hotel or pub in Ireland. Indeed there was a piece in the *Irish Times* the following Monday by someone who had watched the match at ten o'clock in the morning in a bar in Miami in the company of Bono of U2 and a hundred other enthusiasts.

Whatever about Miami, there was a strange mixture of people in the hotel bar in Dundalk. It was not the usual bunch of young adult males; they were probably gathered elsewhere. In fact, there was an equal mixture of men, women and children. But it was the contrast in the children which was most interesting. There were three distinct types all around the same age; the two different reds of Manchester United and Liverpool and the whites. I will come back to the whites later. Many of the young boys were wearing replica soccer jerseys of the teams. In the hierarchy of social status, the more committed and better-off kids had the names of particular players on their jersey. There was one young Manchester United supporter, about nine years old, who not only had "Cantona" emblazoned on his back, but who, in exact imitation of his screen hero playing on the pitch in Wembley, had his hair cut close and the collar of his jersey turned up. I imagined his bedroom full of posters of his star.

I felt sorry for this young boy. Despite his best efforts of imitation, despite his attempts at being ultra-cool, he did not have the same style or swagger of his hero. Times change, but personal inadequacies remain the same. When I was his age, my bedroom was festooned with statues and images of Our Lady. I even had a private altar on my dressing-table which I decorated with fresh flowers. But like the young boy unable to match the Cantona swagger, I could not match the purity, piety and humility of Our Lady.

The tribes

On mature reflection I think that the scene in the hotel represented a moment in time in between the Coliseum in Rome and two opposing tribes doing battle in virtual space. The tribal allegiance was enormously significant. As well as the boys, most of the men present had a strong affiliation with one or other of the teams. It seemed that if their team won, it not only meant that it was the better soccer team, but the glory reflected on them for being followers. But it was not just a soccer superiority. As with most other tribal differences, having beaten one's opponents, there was an associated feeling of moral superiority. This brings us back to the early days of human society and Durkheim's arguments. The sense of social identity and belonging was generated by belonging to a certain tribe. In the classification of the social world, knowing who you were was partly achieved by looking at other tribes and knowing that you were not like them. It would be great if human beings could live in a pluralist world where differences were recognised and accepted. But I get the feeling that with tribes long ago, as with many soccer supporters now, it did not remain at the level of difference. In generating a sense of belonging, loyalty and commitment, tribes convinced themselves that not only were they different, but that they were better. It is no wonder that they had to go and beat the *hell* out of each other.

But social fields such as sport and religion do not necessarily occupy different social spaces or have to be in competition with one another. For a long time in Ireland, there was not just a peaceful coexistence between the Catholic Church and the GAA, but a harmonious relationship which was mutually supportive. The residues of this relationship linger on. And so it was that during the Cup Final I noticed on the counter in the hotel bar there was a collection box for Saint Anthony, and during the match there were girls in their sparkling white Holy Communion dresses running in and out of the bar. These were the supporters dressed in white which I mentioned earlier. What was wonderful and not in the least bit strange was the way these fields overlapped and the way the Red Devils, winners on the day, mixed easily with the white girls dressed for Jesus.

What I am suggesting here is that there is a practical logic to the whole field of following soccer which, like religion, involves affiliations, regular practices, knowing the game and the players, talking about and making pilgrimages to the hallowed turf. However, the main difference between religion and sport is the inability of religion to deliver ongoing regular intensive excitement which binds people together into a united group. As a consequence, religion is not providing the same sense of identity which it used to for many people.

On the same night as the English FA cup final, a teenage girl from Cork died at a rock concert in Dublin. It was an awesome tragedy. There was such a frenzy at the concert that many of those present did not or could not care that people were being crushed to death. But being crushed to death in the name of what? Many adults would never have heard of the Smashing Pumpkins who were playing that night. It was as if a strange religious sect had come to town and unbeknownst to them were able to steal hearts, minds, souls and bodies.

School of Engineering, Trinity College, Dublin.

IN A 16TH CENTURY IRISH UNIVERSITY: 21ST CENTURY KNOWLEDGE.

The Irish.
The Irish have always had a hunger and respect for education. Today, over 40% of our college students choose science and technology.

Ireland.
A member of the European Common Market. Noted for its favorable government attitudes towards business. The most profitable industrial location in Europe for US manufacturers.

Ireland. Home of the Irish. The young Europeans.

IDA Ireland
INDUSTRIAL DEVELOPMENT AUTHORITY

REPUBLIC OF IRELAND

"WE'RE THE YOUNG EUROPEANS".

... the weak link ...

CHAPTER 7

An intelligent island?

JAMES WICKHAM

The Industrial Development Authority advertisement that greeted visitors at Dublin airport used to carry the slogan "Ireland – powered by people". The election leaflet of a recent government minister claimed that the Republic's education system is the best in Europe. Ireland is seen to combine high technology industry (electronics and computer software) with expanding culture industries (film, music and video) to become an "intelligent island". The booming *Celtic tiger* economy is assumed to be based on our wonderful educational system.

Education and economic success

And in many ways Ireland does appear as an educational success story. Over the last thirty years, Irish educational participation rates (the proportion of the age cohort in specific forms of education) have first caught up with and then overtaken not only British ones but also those of some other countries. Participation in education up to the end of second level is high in Ireland and more eighteen and nineteen year olds are in full-time education than in other advanced capitalist societies.[1]

---

1   Organisation of Economic Cooperation and Development, *Education at a glance: OECD indicators*, Paris: OECD, 1996

Yet, just because people go to school or even university does not necessarily mean they learn anything. Researchers have therefore been trying to assess educational achievements by measuring students' literacy, mathematical ability and scientific knowledge. In these terms also Irish schools do perform relatively well. In the most recent international mathematics and science performance test (the Third International Maths and Science Study), Irish school students aged thirteen score higher than both US and German school students.[2]

At third level too, Irish graduates seem to compare favourably with those from many other European countries. For example, in Italy simply passing the school leaving examination gives the right of entry to university, where education is almost free. The result is predictable. The public universities are under-funded and over-crowded, and private fee-paying universities offer the only hope of competent teaching and a qualification with some value. Since entry to third level in Ireland is selective, we have, so far at least, avoided the disasters of Italian universities.

Yet, such indicators say little about how (or even if) formal knowledge contributes to economic growth or indeed to broader social development. The effectiveness of educational spending depends in part on the links between the educational system and the economy. I want to argue that in Ireland such links are weak and/or narrow. When links are *weak*, education and economic activity have very little to do with each other; when links are *narrow*, individual firms relate to individual educational institutions (such as colleges) but not to the wider educational system.

The national innovation system

The contribution of education to economic innovation, in the form of new products and processes, can be analysed through the concept of the *national innovation system*. This concept

---

2 "World education league, who's top", in *Economist*, March 29, 1997

was developed within economic sociology and institutional economics. It was first used in relation to Ireland by Mjoset in his study for the National Economic and Social Council.[3] He argued that the poor innovation record of Irish indigenous firms must be explained in terms of the innovation system within which they are located. Irish indigenous firms have few links either to each other or to education and training institutions; innovation, such as it is, occurs within the foreign-owned sector. As we shall see later, the idea of a weak national system of innovation can be used to explain many other features of Irish education.

In terms of the contribution of education to developing a skilled labour force, a useful general concept is that of the *learning society*. Once again, more is involved than just the number of people in educational courses. A learning society is one in which education is not only a lifelong activity, but one in which learning is interwoven with other areas of life. In a learning society, work involves continuous re-training, recycling, re-learning. As I shall now argue, although in Ireland we have a lot of education, we are not a learning society.

Clearly economic growth depends partly on innovation, that is to say on new products and new processes; this applies to services just as much as to manufacturing industry. The question is how such innovation occurs. In the past, it was understood in terms of technology push. Innovation was assumed to start with scientific discoveries in pure research which then moved down via technological applications into the economy. There is a one-way flow from Research, Technology, Products and Processes to Market.

By contrast, contemporary approaches assume that innovation is fundamentally an incremental process stemming from the interaction of producers, suppliers and education and training institutions. Like learning, innovation also involves doing: in certain situations, people who are making

3 Lars Mjoset, *The Irish economy in comparative institutional perspective*, Dublin: National Economic and Social Council, 1992

things or providing services work out new ways of working. They innovate. This may well stimulate the more formal search for new technologies and raise new questions for scientific research. New products and processes develop through a series of feed-backs. These linkages can take many forms. Some market relationships between firms, in particular ones that are long-term and trusting, can also be channels of information. If skilled people move from one firm to another, or between education and research institutions and firms, then ideas and experience move with them. Social links between managers and entrepreneurs are another obvious source of exchange. Formal institutional structures such as trade associations and chambers of commerce can also be important.

Once innovation is seen in this way, as occurring in a social context, then two consequences follow. Firstly, innovation can no longer be assumed to follow a single pre-determined path. Instead, innovation is shaped by the specific institutional context and develops its own trajectory. Secondly, and directly relevant to understanding the role of education, one can study the extent and content of these formal and informal linkages within which innovation occurs. In particular, if there are strong linkages creating national networks of producers, customers and educational institutions, then we can talk of a strong national system of innovation.

The weak link

The lack of education-economy linkages is suggested by the irrelevance of much Irish education to the growth points of the Irish economy. For example, for all the recent expansion of the Irish software industry, information society issues have hardly been taken seriously in Irish education. In 1996, only sixty-five per cent of national schools had any computer at all, and only twenty-six per cent had acquired these with Department of Education funding.[4] As for the universities,

---

4 Information Society Steering Committtal, *Information Society Ireland: strategy for action*, Dublin: Forfas, 1997, p 38

research for the Computer Applications for Social Scientists (CASS) programme has shown that the number of personal computers (PC) per student ranges from a high of one PC per every ten students in Dublin City University and University of Limerick to a paltry one per thirty in Trinity College Dublin. All way below the Council of Europe recommended level of one PC per every three students! Typically, the recent government White Paper on Education discussed the Irish language and equality of opportunity in great detail but devoted not a single sentence to information technology. And this lack of strategy pervades the entire system. The CASS research has shown that not a single university manager of computer facilities is able to identify a strategy for the pro-vision of Information Technology for undergraduates or identify the forms of usage of existing equipment.

The school system remains dominated by those formal knowledges required for university entrance, rather than vocational and workplace relevant knowledges. The only real criterion of educational success is entrance to third level (the annual Leaving Certificate hysteria), and like the Japanese system this focuses on rote learning. Compared to Holland or Denmark for example, Irish school students are extremely unlikely to take vocationally relevant courses. In Japan, the academicised rote learning of secondary education is counter-balanced by the Japanese employment system with its enormous amount of in-firm training. By contrast, Ireland's *Japanese* secondary system leads to the old-style *British* in-firm training system, that is to say no training at all. Irish firms, and this includes firms in the foreign owned sector, spend 1.2 per cent of sales revenue on training, while the European Union average is three per cent.[5] Equally most FÁS expenditure (Training and Employment Authority) is concentrated on job creation schemes which do nothing to upgrade the skills of those already in work. Its main inter-vention for those in work is the Training Support Scheme,

---

5 *ibid*, p 39

which as of 1996 was absorbing less than two per cent of its total budget. Despite educational advance, this is hardly a learning society!

Almost alone amongst OECD countries, the Irish third level budget provides no resources at all specifically for research; the Irish government spends less on third level research as a percentage of Gross National Product than any other OECD country. And as the recent CIRCA report also documents, this disinterest in research pervades the third level system. Not only is there no institutionalised national system of research evaluation, but not even a single university senior manager is able to identify his or her university's research priorities or even identify its research strategy. Irish scientific researchers, just like Irish technologists, have to emigrate to build a career. CIRCA reports a US professor:

> From time to time, one encounters Irish scientists of considerable talent – usually based in some other country. I suspect that one could assemble at least one more first class university in Ireland if only one could repatriate the best people who have gone abroad for the faculty.[6]

Yet Irish universities do undertake research. The simplest way to measure scientific output is by bibliometric measures, counting the number of papers published by researchers. In these terms, Irish university research output has been expanding faster than both the world and the UK average since the 1980s. The impact or importance of the research can be crudely measured by counting how frequently the papers are cited by other researchers in the world in their own publications (the *citation count*). In these terms too Irish university researchers are beginning to approach world standards.

This paradox would seem to suggest that an Irish national

6   CIRCA Group Europe, *A comparative international assessment of the organisation, management and funding of university research in Ireland and Europe*, Dublin: Higher Education Authority, 1996

research strategy is not necessary. It suggests that Irish research is doing very well thank you even though, and perhaps precisely because, it is not receiving any government funding or government backing. We have been intelligent enough to build an intelligent island on the cheap!

But such optimism is misplaced: the quantity and even the formal standard of Irish research hides major weaknesses. Because government does not fund basic research, Irish universities rely heavily on European Union research funds. This makes it difficult to develop any coherent research strategy that is related to the needs of the Irish economy and of Irish society. For further funding, universities have been forced into an equally opportunistic dependence on private firms, largely foreign-owned. Such research is oriented to the firms' immediate competitive needs; there is no institutional system that can push research towards either precompetitive research or even, more importantly, towards applied research that will benefit a series of firms within Ireland.

The quantity and even the quality of Irish research therefore does not add up to a strong national system of innovation. The relative under-development of an indigenous innovation system can be seen in the bibliometric data: Irish researchers are as likely as colleagues abroad to joint author papers (joint authorship is a sign of collaboration), but they are less likely than colleagues elsewhere to joint author articles with other researchers from their own country. In other words, Irish researchers' networks lead outside the country; their research bears relatively little relationship to activities within Ireland. Irish research is de-centred, fragmented.

Not a learning society

Returning to the issue of the learning society, similar problems can be seen in technological education as a whole. Undoubtedly, the expansion of technological education has made Ireland much more attractive for various forms of mobile investment. The decision to expand electronics education in the 1980s was one of the most successful policy decisions of the decade.[7] However, the manpower needs of industry tend to be met by either courses that are too general or too specific. If the issue is simply the need for more computer scientists, then courses have little relationship to the actual developments in the industry. Alternatively, universities and regional technical colleges become increasingly willing to adjust or develop courses in line with the "needs of industry", but these needs tend to be articulated by single firms who simply use third level institutions to carry out training in the particular skills they require. Once again the problem is the lack of developed networks (as opposed to individual links) connecting firms and educational institutions.

Firms are not under any pressure to carry out general training themselves. High technology firms in Ireland operate a slash and burn approach to Ireland's much vaunted technological educational system. Rather than training and developing their human resources, they use up the latest products of the educational system, secure in the knowledge that they can easily be replaced by next year's batch of graduates. Certainly, the recent government White Paper on Human Resource Development does propose the creation of training networks of clusters of firms, but there seems little recognition of how firmly entrenched are the current practices.

In summary, Irish linkages between education and economy are few and narrow. As a result, Irish research is either of no particular relevance to Ireland or virtually the private property of individual firms: there is a weak system of national innovation. Equally, there is much education and, at third level, much technologically relevant education. But here too education is either too general or too specific, and in addition, education remains something that happens to young people before they enter the labour market: this is not a learning society. For all the undoubted achievements, we are not yet an *intelligent island*.

---

7 Sean O'Riain, "The birth of a celtic tiger", *Communications of the ACM*, vol 40, 3 (March 1997): 1 1-16

... floating signs ...

CHAPTER 8

Peace Protest as Simulacrum

MICHEL PEILLON

O
n 9 February 1996, the Irish Republican Army
bombed its way out of the ceasefire which had given
peace to Ireland for seventeen months. All over the
country, this dramatic event triggered a sequence of actions
which departed in many ways from conventional protests.
They did so, first of all, by the exuberance of symbols they
produced. Books for peace were signed. Candelit rallies were
held. On 14 February, a students' rally at Queen's University
Belfast lasted 17 minutes to represent the seventeen months
of peace. A minute's silence was respected at workplaces
throughout Ireland. The white peace ribbon was launched,
to be worn by all lovers of peace. Numerous cards and letters,
containing half a million signatures, were sent to the *No
More Violence Campaign*. Peace vigils were organised in many
places. Bells were rung at peace marches and in some cases
white pigeons were released. Peace advertisements, in the
names of local dignitaries, were purchased and published in
Derry newspapers. In Derry again, white paper doves were
distributed to be worn by participants at rallies. In Dublin, a
huge table was erected on O'Connell bridge designed to urge
all parties in the conflict to sit down at the negotiating table.
Well over one million people participated, in one way or
another, in this sequence of protests. Close to fifty separate
occurrences of collective protest were actually recorded during
these two weeks.

Signalling protest

Such protests gave a strong symbolic expression of disapproval and dissatisfaction at a turn of events, which came as a total surprise. They expressed and signified a general desire for peace. They were venting a feeling of anger and frustration. But there was nothing behind such signs of protest, no vital force. These actions were simply signalling that protest was taking place: they had been effectively transformed into signs. The sign of protest stood for the protest itself; it looked like the protest itself, but loosely so, as a representation and an approximation. It had become a simulation of protest, what Jean Baudrillard calls a *simulacrum*.[1] The approximate copy had replaced that which it stood for and which had now been erased, occulted from the world. The sign had replaced the real thing, and the latter had simply waned.

The protests reacted to the ending of the ceasefire and the threat of renewed violence. The peace symbols mirrored each other, pointing at each other in an endless chain: church bells, candlelights, paper doves, white ribbons, etc. Ultimately, of course, the peace protests were targeting the end of the ceasefire and, beyond that, the long-lasting armed conflict. An intense and bloody battle has, for more than twenty-five years, been conducted by paramilitary organisations and the British Army. Such a struggle can certainly not be perceived as merely symbolic. At the same time, none of the parties in the conflict has any illusions about its ability to "win the war"; they have all conceded the impossibility of a military solution to the Northern Irish conflict. The armed conflict has become in this way an element in a large struggle, which is both political and symbolic. It serves to signal resolve and determination, to increase political pressure, to position oneself, to play on international opinion. These armed actions now operate as the means of a symbolic struggle. They no longer make sense as straightforward acts of war, as confron-

---

1 Jean Baudrillard, *Simulacres et simulation*, Paris: Galilée, 1981

tations of armies in which maximum energy is applied to overcome the opponent. To use von Clausewitz's expression, war is politics by another means.

Peace protests related not to the reality of the Northern Irish conflict, but to its symbolism. They did so in a very direct way. The bombs which exploded in London to mark the end of the ceasefire were *just* that: a signal, a way of communicating the end of the ceasefire. The IRA did not follow up this act by a campaign of armed action, either in Britain or Northern Ireland. The end of the ceasefire had been symbolised and signalled. And then, nothing happened for a long while and we were confronted with a *phony war* which was also a *phony peace*. The peace protest did not refer to a return to the armed conflict, but to the sign and, beyond that, the possibility of its return. Peace protests no longer related to real occurences but, fundamentally, to other signs. The signalling character of IRA activity was reinforced when, more than two months later, a small bomb detonated in an empty house in London. This armed action did not, para- doxically, indicate the start of a renewed armed campaign but signalled the ever-present possibility of such a campaign. It meant that such a course of action remained on the agenda of the IRA and that they had retained their capacity to walk this path again. A few days later, another bomb was placed under Hammersmith Bridge in London, but failed to detonate. It was implied by some commentators that the bomb was placed there but deliberately made not to explode. Others intimated that the IRA intended a *spectacular* display. In both cases, the explosions were functioning as signs within a system of signs.

Once protest is used to signify protest, once it has become its own sign, the need to protest no longer exists; it will suffice to signal that one is protesting, without having to engage into the actual sequence of protesting. Protests exhaust themselves in their very act of signalling. As simulacra, they lose any content and do not aim at any precise target. They simply relate to a general longing for peace which, as such, cannot sustain enduring collective action. Actual relations of power or tangible stakes in the confrontation were absent in these protests. Nobody lost or won, simply because these actions did not participate to an actual conflict or confrontation of wills. It was not possible to determine if the protest had proved successful or not, if it had achieved its goals, for the latter remained diffuse and lacked specificity. The absence of a subsequent armed campaign by the IRA did not point to the effectiveness of the movement or to its failure. The protests did not belong to strategic moves and they were not sited in power relations. If by power one means the application of resources and energy to achieve one's goal, then power was not being exercised in these protests. They exuded no great sense of opposition, of struggle. Resources were being used in these protests simply to signify protest. Ultimately, this kind of simulated protest developed because a demand existed for it: a demand for an expression of protest which fell short of an actual protest, a protest without a clear target or stake, without power relations and strategic moves.

Implosion

Baudrillard points to an intriguing feature of *simulations*: they absorb a high level of real energy, but this energy is never externalised, never given back. In the same way, the peace protests which occured at this time did not display a high level of energy. New organisations were created for this purpose and old ones were revived. Large masses of people were involved. Yet all this energy produced rather subdued rallies, candlelit marches, parades of people adorned with white ribbons and paper doves. At no stage did one observe an *energizing* of the protests. Baudrillard uses the term *implosion* to refer to such a situation. Implosion indicates a bursting of force which is directed inwards. In other words, the energy which was absorbed by this form of collective action was not externalised and, instead, was compressed inside. This compression and bursting inwards broke down internal barriers and boundaries. The boundary which structured them and, in a fundamental way constituted them,

94

was eradicated. The peace rallies managed to include both those who protested against the end of the ceasefire and those at whom the protest was loosely directed. War is, after all, usually pursued in the name of peace. Members of Sinn Fein openly participated to many of these peace protests and denounced the lack of progress in the negotiations. A suspected high-ranking IRA member conspicuously wore the peace ribbon. The very people at whom the peace protest was directed were able, quite comfortably, to join in these rallies, perform the relevant symbolic acts and demand peace. This ambivalence displayed the indetermination of the aims associated with such actions and the rather loose and diffuse targeting which characterised them. The offenders and those protesting at the offence were brought together in the very act of protesting at the end of the ceasefire. The energy which had gone into such protests did not and could not come out: it simply burst in and was dissipated.

The fickleness of peace protests

The sequence of peace protests we have been analysing provides quite a clear example of what Baudrillard calls simulacrum. They display the four main features which mark such a simulation:

> such protests have been transformed into signs, and the copy comes to replace the protest of reference

> they are inserted within a system of signs, in which they cease to refer to an external reality and respond, instead, to other signs

> they fail to retain the consistency of collective action and cease to operate as effective and substantial protests

> they experience an implosion, in which the divergent poles come into contact: the energy which has been absorbed simply breaks down the internal barriers

and boundaries according to which the phenomenon of protest was structured.

Once the peace protests had been constructed into signs, into simulacra, they could only exhaust themselves and quickly disappear. They will emerge again, triggered by some other signs to which they relate. This has been, so far, the story of the peace movement in Ireland.

... explicit ...

CHAPTER 9

From Sexual Repression to Liberation?

TOM INGLIS

One Halloween in primary school, when I was nine years old, I wrote a message on a piece of paper and sent it around the class: "Do not kiss your girlfriend tonight, there is danger under her lips". When it got to Michael Flaherty, he roared laughing. Brother Bernard was down on him in a flash. Where did the message come from? A quick reign of terror began. I surrendered. He started to beat me with his leather. Suddenly he seemed to realise that it was far too grave a matter for him to deal with. He went and got the headmaster. He came and dragged me down to his office. There he took out his cane and started walloping me as hard as he could. He was a small fat man and soon he had exhausted himself. He gasped for air. "How could I have learnt to write such a thing?" he asked. Thinking rapidly, I blurted out that a Protestant boy had told me. The beating stopped immediately. When he had calmed down, he talked to me about keeping bad company.

Outside language

What was going on then? Was he taking his sexual frustration out on me? Was it sadism, or child sexual abuse? Was beating

99

me some perverted form of pleasure? The reality is that we were both players in a system of sexual discipline, instituted back in the nineteenth century, which controlled sex by silencing and denying it.

My youth was a time when fear and shame about sex mixed uneasily with innocence and ignorance. You could laugh, giggle and tell dirty jokes. But it was difficult to be serious about sex without getting flustered and going red in the face with embarrassment. Sex was outside the realm of normal, everyday language.

I picked these things up at home. I remember watching a play on BBC television with my father. There was a scene in which a couple kissed each other. But this was no Hollywood meeting of pursed lips. This was a long, deep into the mouth event with accompanying hands undoing clothes. My father became very agitated. Eventually he got up from his chair, went over and changed the channel and walked out of the room. We never mentioned or talked about sex in our house.

I remember; you remember; we all remember those days of guilt and sexual repression. It was a time of modesty, chastity and purity of mind and body. Temptation lurked around every corner. It was crucial to avoid bad thoughts and occasions of sin. The slightest thing, an ad for a woman's bra or even the mere mention of the word "sex", could incite passions and lead to sins of concupiscence. As an ordinary player in the teachings, rules and regulations of the Catholic Church, it did not take me long to realise that it was sins against the sixth commandment (*Thou Shalt not commit adultery*) which caused most offence.

It was a time of ignorance. My mother did not tell me the facts of life. But she must have thought that I was spending too much time in the bathroom because she left a Catholic pamphlet for me in there one day. It was full of weird and obscure language, but short on detail. The only formal sex education I received was in my final year in university. I think that was because I was a social science student and it was important to know about these things, especially if you were going to do social work.

The facts of life

But it was not just me. Silence and ignorance about sex had profound social effects. Social research indicates that many Irishmen and women grew up with little or no knowledge of "the facts of life". What was the effect of this? We can only speculate. What we do know is that, in comparison with other Europeans, fewer Irish people got married. Did fear and ignorance of sex contribute to this? One of the ways of controlling population growth in Ireland, which became a major issue after the Famine, was to control the number who got married. The repression and denial of sex, the instigation of awkwardness and embarrassment between the sexes, was part of this process.

Another (demographic) fact of Irish life was that couples tended to be older when they got married. Women were often in their late twenties, early thirties. Nevertheless, Irish women ended up having more children than women in other European countries. To what extent had this to do with ignorance about the facts of life, fear about sex and an inability to talk openly about sexual problems? Perhaps husbands and wives did not have the language or competence to limit or stop having children. But the solution was not exactly in their own hands. Whatever the problem, it had to be presented to and discussed with the doctor and/or the priest who, talking and working together, wrapped and presented the solution within Catholic theology. Many women continued to have children well into their forties. There is evidence that some women, particularly those over the age of thirty-five, began to limit or stop having children. What we do not know is how this practice was negotiated with husbands. How did women, as mothers and guardians of the Catholic faith, limit their fertility when doing so was contrary to Church teaching, when there were no contraceptives available and when there was no talk about sex? Maybe it was silent, solitary, struggle.

Silence and ignorance had other effects. Today I read about how a young teenage girl was regularly raped by her uncle in her bedroom while her mother was downstairs knowing, but

101

denying, what was going on. Over the last ten years there has been a stream of stories about young children being abused, raped, buggered by fathers, uncles, priests, teachers. What was supposedly a time of blissful innocence was for many children a reign of terror. The home which was supposed to be a sanctuary, a safe haven from the outside world, was a torture chamber.

A new regime of sex

This helps remind us, as Foucault[1] has pointed out in the first volume of *The History of Sexuality,* that it was not so much that sex did not exist or was repressed in the past, but rather that in Ireland it operated within a different regime, with a different language and practice. There was a different way of seeing, understanding and relating to sex and the body. But sex was very real and demanding and it was rigorously inculcated in everyone's mind, heart and body. It was deployed in every church, school, hospital and home in the country. It existed in the demands of leading a pure, virtuous and chaste life. The achievement was a fear, guilt and shame about the body, its pleasures and desires. Modern Irish souls were constituted in the panoply of rules and regulations devised around the sixth commandment. Sex was constituted as a danger which lurked in every look, thought, act, word and feeling. It had to be guarded against through constant prayer and a strict regulation of bodies. It had to be sought out and extracted from children and adults in an ongoing process of vigilance, supervision, self-examination and confession.

Times have changed. Today there is a new language, a new way of seeing and understanding sex. Different stories are being told and different people are telling them. Instead of screaming silently, people are now talking openly about

---

1 Michel Foucault, *The history of sexuality*, vol 1, Harmondsworth: Penguin Books, 1981

their problems and what and how they have suffered. Events which were previously denied because they were outside the realm of religious and medical language; because they were deemed preposterous, unthinkable and unimaginable, are now being revealed. They are being told in courts, in newspapers, radio and television, in counseling groups and among friends. A language has been found for what was once inarticulate.

The effects of this new found language have been profound. Anthony Giddens[2] argues that what characterises the modern sexual revolution is people beginning to question and challenge traditional institutions such as religion and medicine. It was people, often women, challenging priests, doctors and other experts which led to a new sexual autonomy of women. The advent of contraception meant that for the mass population of women, sexuality could become separated from a chronic round of pregnancy and childbirth. Although it took place much later in Ireland, the struggle for contraception broke the religious/medical mould in which sexuality had been set. And within sexual relationships, the practice of contraception enabled a new sensibility and intimacy to emerge between women and men. It was this private sensibility which was a crucial catalyst to the challenge of old institutions and the emergence of a new language and public understanding about sexuality, and which helped bring about changes in the enactment, enforcement and interpretation of laws regarding women and sex.

As well as revealing abuses and perversions which had been swept under the carpet, the new language of sexuality helped people discover the pleasures of sex. It was not just being able to have sex without fear of pregnancy, there was a new pleasure in talking, reading about and looking at sex. Desire and fantasy were liberated from the cells of sin. Being turned on by sex had not only become acceptable, it was

---

2 Anthony Giddens, *The transformation of intimacy*, Cambridge: Polity Press, 1992

deemed good and healthy. Instead of sex being denied and silenced, it is openly embraced. There is a demand to accept diversity in sexual identities, orientations and pleasures from homosexuality to eroticism.

But perhaps, as Foucault suggests, everything may not be rosy in the sexual garden of Ireland. It may be that, far from being liberating, the pursuit of sex and the demands of being sexually active and attractive constrain and repress us just as much, if not more, than before? Maybe being sexy does not mean the end of repression, but the instigation of a much more subtle, more penetrating and lasting form of self-discipline, exploitation and social control?

Instead of the priest examining our consciences, we have analysts, counsellors, therapists and psychiatrists helping us to overcome our sexual inhibitions. Television programmes guide us to having good sex. The message is simple. Unless we are easily stimulated, getting it regularly and having good orgasms, there is something wrong with us. The pious, virtuous woman is now seen as sexually dysfunctional. The pure chaste Irish mother of old is now seen as an unresponsive woman suffering from vaginissimus. Madonna has replaced Our Lady.

Sexual constraints have changed from being external under the supervision of priests and doctors, to more internalised forms of self-restraint. But internalised self-restraint may be more repressive than liberating. Are the dietary regimes of the modern barbie girl any less strict than the fasting and abstinence Catholics used to endure during Lent? Is the training regime to develop a fit, lean and healthy body any less harsh than it was to develop a good soul through the penitential practices of Lough Derg and Croagh Patrick? Is the obsession with mortifying the body and denying oneself pleasures all that different from what Matt Talbot used to do to purify his soul? Is confessing sexual sins to Oprah Winfrey any more beneficial than it is to confess to a priest?

TOWARD A REFLEXIVE IRELAND?

... needing a new way ..

CHAPTER 10

Blood

PADDY O'CARROLL*

T he broader aspects of blood donation have until recently been regarded a concern almost solely of the medical profession. But the blood scandals have been widely reported in the mass media, fuelling grave public concern. An expert group, chaired by Dr Miriam Hederman O'Brien, was asked to enquire into the hepatitis C infection through donated blood. A hepatitis C tribunal was set up in October 1996 and its report was published early in 1997. The reports of both the Expert Group and the Tribunal have shown that the management of donated blood does indeed raise some very technical and scientific issues. Nevertheless, the main outcome of these enquiries has been to alert the public to the fact that the organisational aspects of blood management may be as important as technical practices in ensuring the safety of blood and blood products.

The management of blood

Public debate to date in Ireland has, however, shown little awareness that a major international sociological debate has raged for more than a quarter of a century around this very topic: it is concerned with the relationship between blood

---

*I wish to acknowledge the help of K.J. Healy of the Department of Sociology, Princeton University, in preparing this paper.

quality and the way its collection, processing and distribution are organised. The objective of this essay is, first, to explore the possible implications of this debate for an understanding of the recent Irish experience of the management of blood and, second, to show how thinking about blood can lead us directly to a consideration of some of the most fundamental concepts, such as trust and risk, which are being employed by contemporary sociology in its attempt to understand the nature of society today.

The sociologist's primary interest is in the social factors which affect the availability of blood and the level of risk involved in its use. Trust holds society together and, if the often abused phrase "the fabric of society" is ever to be given substantive meaning, it is most likely to be found in the examination of the role of trust and risk in the exchange of blood.

Though the therapeutic use of blood has been attempted in Europe since the seventeenth century, its successful use is a phenomenon only of this century. The practice has grown rapidly since the mid century as a result of developments such as those in surgery. By the 1970s the use of blood and blood products had become enormous. The demand for transfusions peaked in the US in the 1980s at about four million per year. It has since declined as a result of the fear of blood-transmitted disease. The blood products sector (mainly plasma) worldwide is dominated by a small number of very large US pharmaceutical firms which currently supply about sixty per cent of plasma used in Europe. The importance of blood and blood management is therefore socially central.

Normally, in Europe at least, the recipient of blood or blood products has until recently been able to assume that the gift of blood will be beneficial rather than detrimental. The patient has been able to trust unquestioningly not only the donor but also all of the other social groups along the blood chain. Their duties include checking of the donor's health, testing of the donation for disease and rejection of infected donations, viral inactivation of blood products, proper follow-up in the administration of the blood and subsequent checking of the patient for adverse reactions.

The gift of blood

Despite the investment of vast sums in research, particularly in the US, blood cannot yet be reproduced. The corollary of this fact is that the need for blood forces even the most reluctant to recognise the common bond of humanity. This recognition of social interdependence, along with the strong widespread sentiments that the human body and its parts, including blood, are inviolable have ensured that the communal dimension of blood has always been recognised. The majority of Europeans feel that the giving of blood should be a purely altruistic act, and only one per cent feel that it should be treated as a commodity.[1] Even in the most market-oriented cultures, this communal dimension of blood has been recognised.

Given the predominance of the impersonal market as a form of exchange in the contemporary world, the practice of blood donation is all the more remarkable. Today the exchange of presents, at birthdays or Christmas particularly, is one of the last vestiges of a time when, prior to the emergence of the market, the exchange of gifts was the major vehicle for the creation and maintenance of social relationships. Those to whom we give presents are known to us on a face to face basis and we expect that our gift will be returned in one form or another.

The unique character of blood donation as a form of exchange, in contrast, is that it is a free gift to unnamed strangers in which there is "no formal contract, no legal bond, no situation of power, domination, constraint or compulsion, no sense of shame or guilt, no gratitude imperative, no need for penitence, no money and no explicit guarantee of or wish for a reward or a return gift".[2]

Giving blood as a practice is, in fact, such a paragon of social

1 Eurobaromater 41.0, *European blood*, prepared for the European Commission by INRA (Europe), European Community, 1995
2 Richard Titmuss, *The gift relationship*, London: George Allen and Unwin, 1970, p 89

virtue that it could not but be appropriated as a symbol in the ideological battles of the 70s between the supporters of the welfare state and those of the market. This is exactly what happened in 1970 when Titmuss wrote *The Gift Relationship*, in which he contrasted the virtually disease-free blood of the national health system in Britain with high rates of infection (mainly hepatitis), and vast wastage of blood and blood products in the US. Because the former was based almost completely on the contribution of voluntary community donors and the latter depended to a considerable extent on the purchase of blood, he argued that a system of voluntary donation produced blood which was more disease free.

Although on the ideological front the book could do little against the full gale of Thatcherism in Britain, it came as a bombshell in the US, both ideologically and technically. Laxity in the blood business, very high rates of transfusion-induced illness, wastage and shortages created by competition in the market were exposed.

In addition, it quickly became evident not only that the government made no attempt to regulate the privately owned blood bank sector, but also that it had almost no information about it. In consequence, the US set to and overhauled the system with strong encouragement from the state. By the end of the 70s the collection of whole blood had moved almost completely to a *voluntary* donor system (US donors expect some gift in return). Round one to the supporters of the communal principle.

Differing organisational responses to the threat of AIDS

However, the contrast between the response of the voluntary whole blood sector and the blood products (mainly plasma) sector, which paid its donors, to the arrival of AIDS in the early 1980s raised questions concerning the assumed intrinsic connection between voluntary giving and safe blood. The not-for-profit whole-blood sector, having built a strong relationship of trust with its communal suppliers, was initially reluctant to subject them to a screening process (by use of questionnaire) designed to identify high risk groups.

On the other hand, because the relationship of the commercial blood product sector with its donors was purely financial, it was able to pick and choose. If one group was excluded, another could be found quickly. Unlike the not-for-profit sector, they did not have sole responsibility for quality control. Their buyers, often government agencies, were knowledgeable about differences in quality. They thus embraced screening more avidly lest any competitor achieve an advantage. The not-for-profit sector providing whole blood was largely self-regulating and not exposed to the discipline of either state or market. As local monopolies, cartelised nationally and exempt from most consumer suits, they fought shy of public scrutiny. Their initial inclination was essentially to deny that AIDS was a threat to blood safety. Attempts to implement screening, they felt, would call attention to the danger of infection and thus frighten both donors and users of its products. After the development of the AIDS antibody test in 1985, they sought to assure the public that the risk of AIDS by transfusion was much lower than the statistics warranted.[3]

The lessons to be learned from round two of this debate are that there is a dark side to the use of communal ideology. When communal or voluntary institutions are regulated by neither state nor market, protection of territory, avoidance of scrutiny, lack of sensitivity to the fears of clients, secrecy, inflexibility to the point of paralysis and inability to respond appropriately to the threat of even cataclysmic crisis may be the result. Voluntary donation may strengthen community but it cannot guarantee the safety of blood.

The Irish case

In Ireland, the situation of the blood system seems to be quite comparable to the not-for-profit section in the US. It

---

3 H. Sapolsky, "AIDS, blood banking and the bonds of community", in *Daedalus*, vol 118, 3 (1989): 145-63

enjoys a monopoly position legitimated by a strong public commitment to the idea that blood, like health insurance, should be a communal responsibility. For many years, it had provided a transfusion service of the highest standard from which it earned a high degree of public confidence and donor support. Also many potential "blue babies" survive today as a result of the use of the anti-d produced from its laboratories.

The position the system occupied, however, is not without its consequences for the nature of its relationships with the public and for its response to uncertainty created by the as yet unidentified hepatitis-C virus. Like all monopolies, it seemed to prefer the quiet life. It practised minimum disclosure, sought to minimise outside control and gave priority to cultivating community support and confidence from the first moment danger signs appeared until long after it was apparent that the biggest health crisis in the history of the state was about to occur.

Donors of plasma, infected patients, their GPs, health boards, hospitals, the Department of Health, the Expert Group Enquiry, the media and the public at large, all appear to have been either refused information or misled by incomplete information, both by the Blood Transfusion Service Board (BTSB) and by the Department of Health. Warning signs from the testing centre in Middlesex and from the general practitioners involved were not acted upon. Either no warning or inadequate warning was given to hospitals, patients and their GPs. All of this control of information was designed to banish doubts and thus protect the organisation and assure its future.

Furthermore, there were considerable delays in taking steps to prevent further infection and to alleviate the sufferings of those already infected. The fact that the state and its servants, after discovering the true source and extent of the infection, were prepared to have it suggested in court that the victims' fate was of their own making shows how far they were prepared to go to protect the organisation.

The ability of the BTSB to control its environment was also seen in the repeated failure of the Department of Health, and its regulatory agencies, to police its activities. It had no difficulty in stymieing the work of the expert group, and then managed to be appointed to police itself. Given such control of the external environment, it is no wonder that it was able to put the survival of the organisation so far ahead of the safety of its product.

Reassessing Titmuss

We are now forced to reassess Titmuss's influential argument that blood systems based on altruism of the community deliver cleaner and safer blood and blood products. The experience of the not-for-profit sector in both the US and Ireland seem to indicate that this is not the case. The very low rate of transfusion-induced infection which he found in Britain could be attributed more to the generally low rate of infection in the community, the care taken with blood from a minority of communities in which infection was known to be endemic and the very high standards of practice in processing blood.

Infection, it appears, can be spread either by altruism or by the pursuit of gain in the market. What Titmuss did not see was that recourse to the community principle can be used by an organisation to prevent change and ignore uncertainty, while failing to minimise the risk of infection. In the Irish case the need to maintain "public confidence" was accorded priority, whereas in the US loyalty to the donor community who had become contaminated caused the hesitation which was fatal.

Ironically, the practical responses to the reduction of hazard which have been attempted, including autologous donations (i.e. having your own blood stored in advance of an operation) and directed donations (i.e. between friends or family) or purchase from a panel of monitored donors, infringe the community ethos.

Blood, trust and risk society

It should not be forgotten in the horror of the disclosures of the blood tribunal that such disasters are themselves a by-product of the march of science. Risk is directly related to this growth in security. The use of blood and blood products has increased longevity and saved countless lives. Exposure to such risks is a key distinguishing characteristic of life in late modernity, hence the sociologists' conceptualisation of contemporary society as "risk society".[4]

Until the disclosures of the blood tribunal, the level of trust in blood in Ireland remained quite high, no doubt due in part to the lack of any regular public information on the rate of infection in Irish blood. As late as 1995, fifty five per cent of the Irish sample in the most recent Eurobarometer report felt that Irish blood was the safest available, a proportion considerably higher than the EU average of forty per cent.

Post-tribunal Ireland will be a fundamentally different Ireland precisely because it will be characterised by a shift from trust in experts and public institutions to the calculation of risk involved in participation in them. This greater reflexivity will lead to an insistence, first and foremost, on greater disclosure of information such as the rate of post-tranfusion infection. As befits information society, such knowledge will no longer be considered the domain only of experts.

The public will also insist that the state fulfil its supervisory duties. The regulation of bodies such as the BTSB will include sectoral political groups (such as Positive Action) and other stake-holders (such as the representatives of the haemophiliacs). In this way society and politics will undergo fundamental change and the community will reclaim its blood.

---

4 Ulrich Beck, *Risk society*, London: Sage, 1992

... the choice is yours ...

CHAPTER 11

Community of Distrust

MICHEL PEILLON

In 1995 and 1996, the glue which had kept Irish society together apparently dissolved: trust broke down. We have been confronted with what could have hardly been imagined a few years ago. The revelation of the many occurrences of incest and severe abuse which take place behind the closed doors of the home has brought to public consciousness an horrific side of family life. The daily disclosures of clerical sexual abuse struck hard at the heart of traditional Ireland. And then, it was no longer safe to put our life in the hands of medical institutions, as some patients were dying of the neglect or incompetence of "caring" agencies. The good, wholesome food of Ireland, which had long been taken for granted, was also deemed harmful and in some cases lethal. Consumption of beef became a risky business, while pork was shot through and through with anti-biotics. With each bite of fruit and vegetables, one could be ingesting a heavy load of pesticides and fertilisers.

The changing nature of trust

Through these crises Ireland is being propelled, at an incredible pace, into what Anthony Giddens has called *high modernity*.[1]

---

1 Anthony Giddens, *The consequences of modernity*, Cambridge: The Polity Press, 1990

He has placed trust at the centre of the transformation of modern societies. He develops the view that trust constitutes a central ingredient of social cohesion; he also contends that the nature of trust is changing. In traditional societies, trust follows the network of face-to-face relations, those of community, kinship or friendship. One trusts what is familiar and this trust is sustained by traditional rules and personal loyalty. The development of the industrial society has brought about what he calls *simple modernity*, in which trust becomes more impersonal. Every day, one trusts the technical competence of other people, the expertise of those who possess the relevant specialised knowledge.

Today, whole populations are learning that experts disagree with each other and have no monopoly of truth. The unreliability of the expert-systems has created the real possibility of a generalised collapse of trust, and has ushered in another stage of modernity: that of high modernity. Trust, no longer automatically given, has to be won and sustained in the light of alternatives. We still depend on abstract and expert-systems, but we are now responsible for the expertise we choose to trust. Trust has become active and entails a constant monitoring and scrutiny; the statements of experts are subjected to critique and appraisal in an on-going institutional way. All social agents, individual or collective, now adopt this critical attitude in which the statements of experts are bracketed and submitted to a kind of permanent doubt. Irish society has been abruptly confronted with the necessity of becoming reflexive and of moving into high modernity. It no longer operates according to fixed rules and regulations, but organises its collective life in the light of the information and knowledge which it produces about itself

Clerical abuses

The Catholic Church does not operate effectively if it does not form a community of trust. The priest in the parish can be a very isolated figure without the trust of parishioners. The Church, through the clergy, reaches individuals in order to ensure that its teaching is followed; it moulds and "normalises" individual behaviour. The shepherding of souls demands that the priest be given access to the inner self of the parishioners, to be monitored and shaped into a christian mould: that of norms and deeply embedded practices which conform to or uphold the moral principles according to which a religion defines itself. Priests possess the expert knowledge which allows them to officiate and mediate between the daily life of parishioners and God's moral order. But they do not enjoy trust on the basis of such an expert function; it must be propped up by face-to-face interaction, by the familiarity which derives from being close to people and caring for them. Clerical practice in Ireland is rooted in such a traditional trust in order to generate the closeness it requires. For this very reason, sexual abuse by clerics, when revealed, strikes at the heart of the system of trust on which the Catholic Church operates. Only a very small minority of priests may have breached this trust and abused the young people to whom they had been given more or less unrestrained access. Such cases nonetheless went beyond the occasional, aberrant episode. Bishop Duffy declared that the morale of priests was battered by clerical scandals; he referred to them as "the clay feet of the Church" (*Irish Times*, 23 March 1995).

The personalised nature of the relationship amongst priests extends to the relations between bishops and their diocesan clergy. The hierarchical relations which exist between them are in some way embedded in a certain familiarity and in personal knowledge of each other. The hierarchy and the community of priests have responded to the disclosure of sexual abuse in a symptomatic way. They must have first reacted with incredulity and denial, for such abuses contravene core values of the Church. But once the reality and extent of such abuse had been acknowledged, it was treated as a aberration, as a kind of momentary disease to be overcome. The bishops turned to other experts, outside their own traditional area of competency, to therapists who would cure the disease and remove this aberration. Deviant or rather "sick" priests were sent for a few months to therapy sessions and, when deemed cured, returned to normal pastoral duties. Cardinal Daly declared that it would be good for the perpetrators of such abuse to confront their own guilty secret and get the therapy and help they needed (*Irish Times*, 5 October 1995). The remark has been made that the abusers were far more likely to be offered treatment than the abused.

We know now that many of these priests have "relapsed" into abusing young boys and girls as soon as they had the opportunity. The Hierarchy has acknowledged that the "expert-system" on which they depended has been found lacking. They trusted an interpretation of deviant priestly behaviour to which counselling and therapy formed the response: but these experts did not deliver. Trust based on familiarity and close personal relations, on easy access to the family, has been seriously damaged; expert-systems have totally failed. Trust can only be reconstructed by embracing what Giddens calls *active trust*. Priests will be far less able than before to rely on an automatic deference and acceptance from parishioners: they need to overcome suspicion or, more simply, caution and win their trust the hard way. The trust of the hierarchy in faulty expertise will no longer shield them from blame. They will have to take responsibility for the kind of expertise they choose to mobilise. In so doing, they will move from both traditional and modern trust to the active trust of late modernity.

Food scares

All expert discourses formulated around food have in the past few years been thoroughly discredited. Assertions which are made about every category of food are contradicted a few months later. Butter has, for instance, undergone a series of metamorphoses from a dangerous substance to "not so bad after all". People who heed the statements of experts experience regular dietary shifts.

In November 1986, Bovine Spongyform Encephatology (BSE or, as it became popularly known, *Mad Cow Disease*) was first identified as a disease; it was recorded in Ireland in

1989. It was then thought that the cattle contracted the disease by being fed compounds which contained offal and bonemeal from sheep infected with scrapies. Consequently, the offal of diseased cows was banned for human consumption or from entering the food chain. Over the years, the number of BSE cases in England increased dramatically: 153,592 cases were officially registered between 1989 and 1995, while only 124 cases were recorded in Ireland for the same period. The number of new cases rose in 1996 to 64 (from 16 in 1995). There exists no clear evidence of the disease being transmitted from cow to calf or from animal to animal in the herd. Nevertheless, a policy of herd slaughtering was adopted in Ireland.

We were of course assured that the disease could not pass the species barrier and that humans simply would not contract mad cow disease from eating infected beef (or in any other way). In March 1996, what had been the steadfastly proclaimed scientific view was abandoned. It was acknowledged that ten people in England had died from a type of Creutzfeldt Jakob Disease (CJD) attributable only to the consumption of infected beef. The BSE crisis broke out when the possibility of such a link was acknowledged by the Minister of Agriculture in the Commons, with an ensuing worldwide ban on British beef export. Politicians mobilised science in an exercise of damage limitation. But their pronouncements and interventions intensified popular distrust. Science was used according to a strange logic: the lack of absolute evidence about such links was interpreted as the absence of such links.

The collapse of the expert system around BSE has generated many responses. In all cases, the responses aimed at restoring some trust. The most obvious response consisted of declarations of reassurance: "Our beef is good for you" or "You can be sure of Irish Beef" (An Bord Bia) represented standard statements by farmers, butchers and politicians alike. Then it was realised that supermarkets shelved hundreds of products containing British beef derivatives. We were quickly assured of the safety of such products.

However, politicians knew that their statements carried little credence: it was not what they were saying which met with disbelief, but the fact that they were saying it. Reassurance would have to come from another source, clearly above suspicion. The government put forward the idea of an independent Food Safety Board, composed of experts and with wide-ranging powers. The Board was established in October 1996, but the definition of its actual functions became embroiled in party politics; its future remains uncertain to this day.

Consumers of beef found their own ways of reestablishing some trust. Many people turned to retailers they had long dealt with. They thought that these retailers had a clear idea of where the meat came from, how it had been produced and processed. Some butchers can issue the required assurances. Several chains of butcher shops or small supermarkets have set up their own quality schemes. They have either bought their own farms and reared the cattle they sell, or else they have imposed clear standards concerning for instance what is fed to the cattle. Butcher shops have retained a significant proportion of the meat market and a return to this kind of personalised shopping is probably more manageable for the sale of meat than for other types of food. But can the regression to a traditional form of trust in shopping be sustained in an era of mass consumption?

Another response consisted in creating a new type of expert-system which would guarantee the quality of the meat. Calls were made for the introduction of a labelling scheme for all beef products, with a display of origin and quality. Such a tagging procedure is used by the two hundred and seventy registered organic farmers, to allow consumers to track the meat back to the producer. Some scientists have been quick off the mark to find a way of tracing meat back to the farm of origin, using DNA samples. They have applied for a patent and set up a company to exploit the method. In May 1997, the Minister for Agriculture and Food announced the introduction of a beef quality assurance scheme which would trace the origin of the meat. It will be based on the mandatory registration of all relevant information about an animal's history: farmers, hauliers and cattle dealers, marts, compound feed and meat processors will have to provide information at each stage. This information will be accessible from a central computer in the Department of Agriculture. Such a "National Beef Assurance Scheme" constitutes a procedure for monitoring the history of an animal and imposing standards. But the monitoring is not directed at consumers as such. Rather, experts, foreign customers and supermarkets will have access to the database. It sets up an administrative expert-system for other relevant experts.

This kind of response involves the elaboration of improved expert-systems which are meant to restore trust. If they succeed in doing so, the need to go further, to move beyond simple modernity disappears. At the same time, such a move facilitates the emergence of a very different kind of situation in which consumers face alternative systems of guarantee. Concerns about the treatment of poultry, for instance, have encouraged the creation of labels of guarantee for free-range eggs or free-range chickens. Similar strategies have been mobilised for organic food. These labelling strategies now belong to a marketing policy of promoting the image of a brand. In the same way, so-called green products have led to interminable claims and counterclaims about damage to the environment. Consumers are faced with a range of alternatives which all rely on alleged expert-systems, and they have to choose between them. The Irish consumer is being forced into the active trust of high modernity. Many people, mainly the young, have used their reflexive capability simply by opting for vegetarian food.

The BSE crisis epitomises the fact that, more than ever before, the consumption of food has become a risky business. The use and abuse of food has always carried its own dangers. But the new risks are more than ever man-made; food is not simply produced, but it is nowadays fabricated. The nature of the new risk is well illustrated in the following statement by the director of the British Consumer Association, and it applies, albeit with less immediacy, in the Irish context:

> Consumers who want to avoid the risk of BSE have no choice but to cut out beef and beef products from their diet. There is currently an unquantifiable risk in eating beef.
>
> Some consumers will decide that the risk is acceptable and our advice to them is that they can reduce the risk by only eating 'muscle meat'.
>
> There is no scientific information available that can predict the level of risk with any security. This poses consumers with a very difficult choice. (*Irish Times*, 23 March 1996)

Dying from eating some types of food has become another risk of modern life which, in the same way as disability or unemployment, is nowadays insured against. A broker offered a lump sum of £25,000 for insured victims of CJD. It seems that if full trust is beyond our grasp, we can nonetheless find ways of accommodating distrust and living with it.

Doubt as the new basis of trust

The trust that people have in their institutions and about each other is being seriously eroded. Two dramatic occurences of trust breakdown have been looked at, and similar considerations apply to the so-called blood scandals. Each situation involved a different mix of traditional and modern trust, one based on familiarity and the other on expert-systems. The Catholic Church, as a community of trust, has clearly been undermined by clerical sexual abuse, for its pastoral work reposes on the personal trust which derives from close contact. Parishioners will monitor the trust they put in their priests; bishops will have to take responsibility for their choice of experts. In the same way, the trust of consumers in beef and food in general has collapsed; they have ceased to rely on automatic expert-systems and have no option but to engage in active trust. There is, in a sense, something reassuring about the disagreement of experts, for it leaves some room for our own judgement. More worrying are those situations in which experts agree.

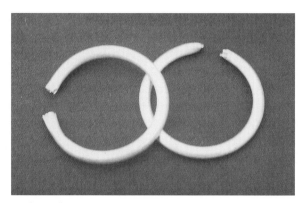

... the split ...

CHAPTER 12

Divorce and Cultural Rationality

MICHELE DILLON

Within the space of ten years, the status of divorce in Irish society has been transformed. In 1986, two-thirds of the Irish electorate rejected a constitutional amendment to allow divorce, whereas in 1995 a majority voted in favor of constitutional change. While the proportion of the electorate who rejected the initiative in 1986 was far greater than the slim majority who endorsed the 1995 proposal, legal divorce is now a sociological reality in Irish society. What are we to make of this social fact? Is it a sign that Ireland has embraced modernity, choosing to join the rest of the Western world by enacting laws that privilege individual freedom over the constraints of tradition, religion and family obligations? Or, is this too simplistic a frame for understanding the symbolic significance of what the Irish have wrought with respect to divorce? These are the questions I would like to address in this short essay.

The modernity of pluralism

On the face of it, it does indeed seem that the shift in the status of divorce is indicative of the social and cultural rationality associated with modernity. Modernity is characterised by an increasing functional differentiation between institutional spheres. Thus the introduction of divorce reflects an increasing autonomy between the institutions of the family and the economy, and between church and state. This differentiation is never as clearcut in practice as in theory. As the 1995 divorce debate highlighted, the economic bases of family relations, and especially the symbolic and material signifi- cance of the *farm family*, endures as a major defining characteristic of Irish society.

Cultural rationality implies that different values inform the norms of behavior across the different spheres of private and public life. For example, the allegedly impersonal and achievement-oriented values of the workplace differ from the more expressive and ascriptive considerations involved in family relations and interactions among friends. It is the differentiation between personal and societal values that legiti- mates an autonomy between the moral and religious views people hold and the laws that they accept and endorse as citizens. Cultural rationality assumes, moreover, a reflexivity about values. This recognises the social context in which specific values emerge, and the fact that not all values are universally shared or shared to the same degree. Thus a society can value both marriage and divorce simultaneously.

In this view of cultural rationality, then, the introduction of divorce is a significant marker of Ireland's modernity. From a society in which the law was seen as the mirror and protector of doctrinally grounded religious values, we now have a situation in which the law is at odds with the values espoused by Catholicism. This disjunction highlights the practical acceptance of cultural pluralism. Although the vast majority of the Irish people continue to be actively involved Catholics, a substantial proportion differentiate their attachment to the values espoused by Catholicism (the indissolubility of marriage) and conflicting values (divorce) that they apparently see as serving the common good of Irish society.

Another manifestation of cultural rationality is the fact that people can believe in a theological tradition and still reject some of its teachings as being unreasonable in practice. Thus, as many Irish (and non-Irish) Catholics construe

Catholicism today, a person can believe in the morality of divorce, and/or be divorced, and still be a "good" Catholic. As in other domains of social life, people use a common-sense approach grounded in their own experiences rather than the authority of elites to determine what is important and what is less central to religious identity.

There is also a third sense in which the enactment of divorce legislation may be interpreted as indicative of cultural rationality. As the 1995 referendum vote highlighted, the legalisation of divorce was a majority but not a consensual stance. A substantial proportion of the Irish people voted against divorce. These people have thus been coerced into accepting its legal status. Yet those who oppose divorce have responded to change by accepting the legitimacy of democratic procedures whilst rejecting the substantive values institutionalised as a result of the democratic process. Other than using legal means to challenge the government's financial role in the pro-divorce campaign, those opposed to divorce have not engaged in civil disobedience or, more extremely, resorted to violence as a means of protesting the (barely) popular will. One might interpret this apparent consent to the new status quo as evidence of a certain political passivity. On the other hand, it seems more likely to be indicative of people's ability to tolerate pluralism – because, after all, opponents of divorce were using political channels to lobby against divorce during the referendum debate. Overall, then, the Irish people as a whole, irrespective of their personal views of divorce, appear to accept that pluralism is, as Chantal Mouffe[1] argues, part of the conceptual definition of modern democracy, and not simply a function of a society's size or demographic composition.

---

1 Chantal Mouffe, "Democracy, power, and the political", in Seyla Benhabib (ed), *Democracy and difference. Contesting the boundaries of the political*, Princeton: Princeton University Press, 1996, pp 245-56

The limits of cultural pluralism

The question remains, however, whether cultural rationality itself should be valued. Does pluralism support or threaten the cohesiveness and integration of a given society? In America, for example, the functional necessity of separating political from religious values, as in the formal separation of church and state, has long been taken for granted. It was well understood that religious and ethnic diversity could incite political antagonisms that might threaten the social order if pluralism was not the framework in which public policies were shaped. The absence of a monopoly church and the cultural legitimacy of several diverse religious denominations implicitly communicates the idea that there is not a single universal Truth, but several different valid moral standpoints.

This is not to imply that ethnic and religious diversity has not historically been a source of conflict in American society. Yet, it was not until the 1960s that cultural diversity appeared to threaten in an unprecedented way the bounds of what had traditionally been understood to be implied by pluralism. Among other emancipatory movements, the women's movement, for example, challenged the moral foundations of a pluralism that forged a national community by denying the full practical equality of women. The success of the women's movement in achieving a broad array of legal and institutional reforms pertaining to education, employment, marriage and reproduction, contributed to transforming the cultural landscape of American society.

In retrospect, however, while celebrating the moral rightness of the push for participative equality, many feminists have expressed concerns about the ways in which equality was institutionalised. In particular, they challenge American society's over-emphasis on the unencumbered autonomy and rights of the individual and its under-appreciation for the necessarily communal or relational contexts in which people must live meaningful lives. They reject the libertarian view that contends that if divorce is an individual's private right, then the personal and economic costs of divorce are also private issues that should be outside the realm of public policies designed to mitigate economic hardship.

Clearly, feminists and social conservatives take contrasting views of divorce, its impact on society, and how it should be regulated. What they appear to share in common, however, is an interest in finding solutions to help contain the communal "disorder" and anomie attendant on the increased autonomy of individual choice. The 1990s are thus being called a period of "moral regeneration" as feminists and communitarians, despite their many differences, seek to establish a new balance between individual rights and social responsibilities.[2] Currently in America, a society which led the way in enacting cultural rationality, cultural pluralism is being recast to take greater explicit account of the shared communal bases of individual and social relations.

The Irish case is obviously very different to that which pertains in America. Whereas American society has given excessive emphasis to individual rights, in Ireland, norms and institutional expectations have over-emphasised communal obligations at the expense of the autonomy of the individual. Given this context, the legalisation of divorce is to be welcomed as one effort to redress the coercive force imposed by appeals to the sanctity of tradition and of religious teaching. It also goes some way towards symbolically mitigating the injustices of previous policies that penalised people, especially women, whose marital circumstances deviated from the normative ideals enshrined in Irish marriage.

It would be unrealistic to expect that a change in the law will automatically transform people's attitudes toward divorce. It is also likely that the socially stigmatised status of those who get divorced will take some time to dissipate. Nonetheless, formal tolerance of divorce may foreshadow and pave the way for further changes in actualising pluralistic

---

2 Amitai Etzioni, *The new golden rule. Community and morality in a democratic society*, New York: Basic Books, 1996

values in other domains of Irish society. We can anticipate, perhaps, a further liberalisation in the status of abortion, and an expansion of the civil rights of gays and lesbians.

It is also apparent that there is some advantage for a society to be a cultural *laggard* in embracing modernity. Ireland's relative tardiness in legalising divorce may well enable Irish society to avoid the excesses of social disorder attributed to divorce and related changes in other western societies. By embracing change at a later time, relative to other societies, the introduction of divorce in Ireland was debated in the context of the alleged positive and negative consequences attributed to divorce in other countries. In the 1986 amendment debate, rhetoric stressing the somewhat exaggerated negative economic consequences of divorce may well have been decisive in accounting for the amendment's rejection by the electorate, and especially its rejection by a disproportionate percentage of women voters.

On the other hand, the 1986 debate paved the way for the subsequent success of the 1995 proposal. In large part because of the 1986 debate, the context of the 1995 debate was one in which people were very familiar with the idea of divorce. In 1986, by contrast, despite the relatively high incidence of broken marriages, divorce was not part of the Irish public (and private) vocabulary. More concretely, the negative scenarios alluded to in 1986 provided a warning to legislators of the sort of threshold any future divorce initiative would have to cross if it was to have a chance of success with the electorate. Accordingly, changes pertaining to property rights and child custody were established prior to the 1995 divorce amendment. The enactment of these specific changes went a long way toward toning down the use of emotionally charged symbolism in the anti-divorce arguments of activists in the 1995 debate.

The relatively restrictive provisions pertaining to getting a divorce in Ireland are obviously disappointing to some couples in terms of their practical implications. Nevertheless, these restrictions serve an important symbolic purpose. As it is formulated, Ireland's definition of divorce communicates an important cultural message. The Irish divorce law recognises the autonomy of the individual and the legitimacy of her/his particular circumstances. At the same time, its imposition of a lengthy pre-divorce separation amplifies the cultural message that marriage should not be abandoned without deliberation. Irish divorce thus recognises individual autonomy while simultaneously protecting the social value of familial and communal obligation.

Each country, of course, must grapple with its own historically embedded cultural tensions. Insofar as the past is a good predictor of the future, it is unlikely that post-divorce Ireland will suffer from the anomie so often associated with other modern societies. The Irish challenge, by contrast, will be how to continue the fight for individual rights against a binding communal tradition so eloquently articulated by the official representatives of both church and state.

... the light of the diaspora ..

CHAPTER 13

Heroes of the Diaspora?

MARY CORCORAN

The frequent representation of successful emigrants in the Irish media – in particular the portrayal of Irish emigrants as adventure-seeking, talented, ambitious and successful – has helped to reinforce a tacit acceptance of emigration among the general public and the political class. The experience of high profile emigrants such as Oliver Tattan, recently returned as the new chief executive of An Bord Trachtala, neatly fits the idea of emigration as a freely chosen course of action. Such a portrayal is favoured by the Irish media. Tattan admitted that in deciding his future, he never gave Ireland a second thought – at least in the short-term. "Coming up from Tipperary, Dublin was seen as the gateway out. I never considered the alternative. I didn't look for jobs here. I wanted to see the world" (*Sunday Business Post*, 8 September 1996). In this case, the adventurer returns to a welcoming reception in the financial press. Yet the same media present no analysis of why the opportunity to return to Ireland coveted by many is, in reality, available only to a few.

Media, emigration and agency

Celebrities make better copy than emigrants on the margins, for whom success has been longer coming, intermittent or has evaded them altogether. Stars from the diasporic firmament are regularly paraded through the media and claimed as *our own*. Paeans to Tony O'Reilly appear in the pages of the many Irish publications under his stewardship. Michelle Smith is transformed, at least in the short-term, into a national hero in the wake of her achievements at the Olympics. Liam Neeson is feted as the original "brainy and brawny" Irish Hollywood star. Frank McCourt, the Pulitzer prize-winner, is invited *home* to take up a post at the University of Limerick. These stars are never referred to in the media in terms of their emigrant status, yet their achievements are attributable to the fact that they have lived and worked elsewhere. O'Reilly, Smith, Neeson and McCourt are treated as *diasporic heroes*, which is conveniently conflated with the concept of national hero. The emigrant part of their identity has been fudged, however, so that we in Ireland can assert ownership of their achievements. They have been promoted to the celebrity subset of Irish emigrants, the transnationally successful elite.

The members of this elite are strategically positioned to enjoy the reflexive project associated with modernity which, Giddens argues, allows individuals to create and sustain their own unique biographical narratives in the context of a myriad of possibilities and choices. By creating identities for themselves that are no longer tied to nationality, family, ethnicity or class; the transnational elite demonstrate their facility to individualise themselves through alternative means. According to Lash and Urry, the presence of information and communication structures makes this process of reflexive individualisation possible.[1] It is significant that our diasporic heroes are drawn precisely from those spheres of life which are deeply implicated in global information and communication structures – transnational media systems, international sport and publishing. However, the ability of

---

1 Scott Lash and John Urry, *Economies of signs and space,* London: Sage, 1994, p 111

individuals to produce their lives in a reflexive way, that is to say to choose according to which narrative they are going to live, is far from being a universal phenomenon. Such an ability is a property of particular positions within society. For the vast majority of Irish emigrants, in the past and the present, it is the structural processes underlying Irish society which have been the key determinants of individual biographies. Like the notion of agency, the idea of reflexivity is deeply seductive, particularly when attempting to construct the image of the Irish emigrant in modernity. The media encourage us to share the glory of Ireland's diasporic heroes vicariously, while simultaneously airbrushing out the much more mundane and much less media-friendly existences of thousands of Irish people around the globe. Michelle Smith's humdrum life in an anonymous housing estate in the Netherlands during the years leading up to the Atlanta Olympics may have been heroic, but it went unrecognised. Success elevated her from the ranks of the emigration statistics to celebrity status as a disaporic/national hero, in the process reducing the emigrant grind that preceded the glory to a scene-setter for a modern fairy tale. This is the story of emigration that the media report, and the one that we want to hear about. The construction of these diasporic heroes as reflexive agents charting their own destinies, provides us with a set of compelling role models to whom we may aspire.

Celebrating emigration

A perennial feature of the Irish cultural and academic calendar is the Summer School, which provides good copy for journalists during the silly season. The musings of a select group of *talking heads* who attend these schools are regularly reported via the media to a wider audience. In 1996, the Parnell Summer School held a symposium on "The Impact of Emigration in Ireland", which was extensively reported in the *Irish Times* (15 August 1996). The report suggested that emigration is now to be welcomed, and quoted a number of speakers to corroborate this assertion. Senator Joe O'Toole informed the symposium that "there is nothing wrong with the fact that 10,000 students would have to go to Britain to study. Let them out there to do the business". The then Senator (and now Deputy) Marian McGennis stated that "the way forward is to invest in children and give them the skills to compete anywhere in the world". Although both commentators are undoubtedly genuine in their views, their pronouncements are more than a little disingenuous. Their approach to the thorny subject of emigration is framed within an exclusive rather than inclusive discourse. In other words, we are encouraged to accept and celebrate the *successful emigrant* or agent, while failing to acknowledge the existence of *the other*. In this context, *the other* represents the marginalised emigrants whose lowly position within the socio-economic structure means that few opportunities are open to them. Both O'Toole and McGennis are reflecting a media convention, of characterising the typical emigrant as skilled, studious, competitive and businesslike. Such a characterisation of emigration as a beneficial experience for the best and brightest, functions as a soothing anodyne, assuaging any doubts we may have about the fate of those who leave Ireland, without credentials, prospects or marketable skills.

Furthermore, by emphasising the individual benefits of emigration for the select few, both politicians and the media deflect attention from the structural weaknesses in the Irish economy which have given rise to historically high rates of emigration in the first place. This most recent obfuscation in evidence at the Parnell Summer School fits neatly into a long tradition in Irish public life of side-stepping the less palatable aspects of emigration. Policy-makers, politicians and, more recently, the media have demonstrated a marked preference for agency-level rather than (the much more complex) structural-level explanations of social processes such as emigration. There is a clear tendency to portray emigrants as goal-oriented actors, who can be eulogised as highly motivated adventurers willing to tackle any challenge. The more the emigrant can be construed as a path-breaker, conquering frontiers far afield, the less we have to dwell on why he or she left in the first place. Structural factors which underpin relatively high rates of emigration – especially when compared to our European partners – have largely remained unexamined, because emigration has tended to be interpreted as a matter of free choice. In a similar vein, the media have recently latched on to the notion of the *Celtic Tiger*, portraying Ireland as the economic powerhouse of Europe. There has been almost no interrogation of the fact that unemployment and rates of emigration among certain categories of the population remain at higher levels than the majority of our counterparts within the European Union. Once again, politicians are engaging in a glossing exercise with which the media seem all too willing to collude.

No one can deny the individual benefits which may accrue from emigration: better work opportunities, valuable new experiences and the development of expertise, to name but a few. However, by framing the debate in those terms, the collective necessity of emigration for those who see no place for themselves in Irish society is consistently underplayed. To define emigration simply as a "biographical narrative" freely chosen by reflexive agents is to seriously misread the total picture. It may be a lifestyle alternative for celebrities, and for a professional and skilled elite, but for those whose decision to leave is dictated by the increasing flexibilisation of the international labour market, emigration can and does involve dislocation, exploitation and marginalisation.

The fact is that emigration in the late twentieth century is a complex and multi-dimensional phenomenon. Whereas once emigrants were drawn almost exclusively from the agricultural and labourer classes, nowadays emigration permeates the entire social class system. The motivation for leaving is not always economically determined, since people also leave for personal and political reasons. It is not an accident of fate that a large population of Irish HIV/AIDs sufferers live in London. Nor is it coincidental that so many Northerners are resident in the major cities of the United States. Just as we have had trouble facing up to the economic realities which underscore high emigration, we have been reluctant to analyse the social and cultural factors which encourage people to emigrate.

Irish emigrants are well represented among a vast army of skilled and semi-skilled labour which crisscrosses the globe. Despite the decline in net migration figures, Ireland still experiences a significant outflow. One hundred and seventy-seven thousand people left Ireland in the five-year period from April 1991 through April 1996. About two-thirds of those were in the 15-24 age group.[2] At a 1997 conference on emigration organised by the Emigrant Advice Network, Sr Joan Kane of the Federation of Irish Societies in London remarked that Irish agencies in Britian have seen no decrease in the numbers contacting their services. On the contrary, there has been an increase in the range of problems with which service providers have had to contend. Irish emigrants still queue outside the Cricklewood Cafe in London for a day's casual labour. The scene is the same as that faced by earlier generations, but the context has changed. Deregulation of the industry has made construction work even more precarious than it was before. Nowadays, Irish emigrants compete with Bosnians and Romanians on the hiring line. Irish emigrants are increasingly incorporated into a globalised labour market which is characterised by worsening pay and conditions, increased ethnic competition, conditions of work which are contingent, and tenuous legal status.

Is emigration really good for us? Irish people still face prejudice and discrimination in British cities. While the majority of Irish in Britain may not be confronted with overt racism on an ongoing basis, we know that racist attitudes can become institutionalised over time. And institutionalised racism is much more difficult to identify and challenge. Racism against Irish people is not just confined to paddy-whackery or the use of racial epithets among construction workers on building sites. A number of recent cases taken by

2   Central Statistics Office, *Annual population and migration estimates, 1991-96,* Dublin: Dublin Stationery, October 1996

the Commission for Racial Equality in Britain have proved that prejudice and discrimination against Irish people persists even in middle-class workplaces. Racism operates at a much deeper level than that we are exposed to in the British tabloid press. There is, for example, widespread discrimination against the Irish community in the British Criminal Justice System. A recent report concludes that persons of Irish descent are more likley to be stopped by the police in inner cities than any other ethnic group, they are most likely to be the victim of a street crime and are disproportionately represented among alleged miscarriages of justice. Furthermore, the report also found that the Irish are disproportionately represented among the homeless, the unemployed and the mentally ill. Groups such as these are more likely to be in conflict with the criminal justice system and are already subject to prejudice and discrimination.[3]

While emigration can offer the possibility of making a living to many, and unimagined economic opportunities to the select few, there is emerging evidence that it may have a detrimental impact on both physical and psychological well-being. A recent report by the International Organisation for Migration demonstrates that Irish emigrants die earlier and suffer from higher rates of disease than the native born populations of their host countries. These higher rates of morbidity and mortality seem to be carried through to subsequent generations. These are the less palatable aspects of emigration which we, here in Ireland, seem increasingly hesitant to interrogate.

Emigration as an adventure in global space

To return to the talking heads at the Summer School, Olive Braiden addressed the symposium suggesting that for Irish

---

3   Action Group for Irish Youth, The Bourne Trust, Federation of Irish Societies, Irish Commission for Prisoners Overseas and National Association of Probation Officers, *The Irish community: discrimination and the criminal justice system*, London, 1997

emigrants "the sense of alienation is no longer what it was before the days of satellite, the Internet and the cheap phone call". It is true that the availability of modern technology – which of course is not equally available to all – can alleviate some of the loneliness associated with separation from family and community. Ethnic groups now constitute electronic communities which link the diasporic population with those they left behind. In accepting the All Ireland Football honours in 1996, the captain of the Meath team explicitly (and very naturally) acknowledged the audience viewing the proceedings on satellite around the world. Being privy to an event is not the same as being present at an event, however. Relocation always involves dislocation, whether that dislocation is manifest or latent. When Irish emigrants go abroad, they assiduously set about creating and participating in ethnic communities, in part to counteract the pervasive sense of dislocation. These ethnic communities are powerhouses of activity – economic, political and social. Ethnic entrepreneurs generate jobs, ethnic brokers place people in jobs, and emigrants spend their wages in the ethnic communities. They live and socialise locally, sustaining local ethnic enclaves in global cities. The attachment to the ethnic community recreates for them, at some distance, a home from home. These are agents actively reproducing social structure through processes of interaction. Virtual communities – such as those offered through telecommunications and the Internet – can only mimic the real thing. Real familial and communal closeness is an intensely physical as well as psychological experience. Globalisation has not eradicated the crucial importance of family and locale in our self-identification. Cultural rites of passage lose their intensity of emotion and sense of communality when the parties to such events are scattered worldwide. Emigrant alienation does not disappear, it simply gets expressed in different ways. Perhaps it is the sublimation of this alienation which is contributing to the higher rates of morbidity and mortality among Irish emigrants and their descendants.

I recently shared a Thanksgiving Dinner with some Irish

emigrants at a local bar in an Irish community in New York City. Thanksgiving Dinner is a quintessentially American phenomenon, which brings together family members in a great and gluttonous harvest feast once a year. Ten young Irish people from the same town in Ireland, several siblings among them, shared rubber turkey and processed peas in a pub whose ambience provided a somewhat less than authentic backdrop to the proceedings. Over the tasteless dinner, the symbolic significance of which was soon forgotten, these young people talked endlessly about what was happening in Ireland. Their hunger was not for turkey and pumpkin pie but for news and analysis of the goings on at home. They fell eagerly upon every titbit offered by the visitors present. They rehearsed the journeys back to Ireland that they planned to make at Christmas. They seemed to be living to return so that they could return to living.

Politicans and policy-makers have traditionally opted to present *the problem* of Irish emigration in terms of agency, while underplaying the importance of structural factors in shaping the experience of Irish emigrants. In the age of the soundbite and personality journalism, the media increasingly employ an *agency spin* in packaging their reporting of emigration, which emphasises the importance of people as architects of their own destinies. The agency model of emigration which prevails is most clearly expressed in the media celebration of diasporic heroes. At the same time, we recoil from images and stories of Irish diasporic communities which reflect a different reality.

LIMITS OF MODERNITY

... the new age ...

CHAPTER 14

New Age Travellers on *Cool* Mountain

CARMEN KUHLING

In the past few years, several public figures have spoken out against New Age Travellers in Ireland. For example, the business people of Dunmanway have criticised them for being "dirty and a possible health risk", claiming that "their children run around with practically nothing on", and that most of them live in "shacks and dilapidated cottages" (*Southern Star*, 18 January 1997). Similarly, Senator Michael Calnan has denounced the "appalling conditions" in which some Travellers live (*Cork Examiner,* 22 April 1997). Much of this coverage has gone to great lengths to construct New Age Traveller lifestyle as a threat to the well-being of the surrounding communities, drawing attention to how Travellers "flout the law", "rip off" the social welfare system, and present a "health risk" and "disease hazard".

Threat to the order of modernity

A deeper reading of these concerns illustrates that the real anxiety expressed about the New Age Travellers is not based on their potential threat to public health, but rather their potential threat to the moral order of modernity. An analysis of newspaper accounts which report various public criticisms of New Age Travellers reveals that the concerns expressed about the possible health hazard New Age Travellers pose masks a more covert agenda of moral regulation. Such accounts suggest that the real anxiety around New Age Travellers is not about the possible risk they pose to the health of local citizens – they suggest rather a more amorphous fear of *moral* contamination posed by this different way of life. For instance, Councillor Pat Murphy's claims regarding the "disease risk" of living in unhygienic conditions mask his real concern: that there is "no law and order for these people" (*Cork Examiner,* 22 April 1997). Although Senator Michael Calnan implies that his concern is for the effects of New Age Travellers on local residents, his real anxiety seems to be New Age Travellers' appearance, claiming that they are not "presentable" and that, as a result of their presence, the town of Dunmanway "begun to look ugly" (*Southern Star,* 18 January 1997).

However, a much more fruitful response to the various ways in which New Age Traveller lifestyle flouts some of the conventions of modernity is to try to understand the meanings that such a lifestyle has for members of this community. Several New Age Travellers I spoke with, living in West Cork and Clare, described themselves as self- proclaimed refugees from Thatcher's Britain, from the dismantling of the welfare state, from the introduction of the Public Order acts, the unemployment crisis, and the clampdown on squatters rights. Others claimed more generally to be refugees from the city, perceiving themselves as damaged by the fragmentation, the complexity, and the intensity that characterises the contemporary urban experience. Some conceived of their pilgrimage to rural Ireland as a retreat from urban life, as a quiet place to recover from the excesses of modernity: from personal crisis, assaults, substance abuses, and other traumas associated with modern life.

Refugees from modernity

Although their self-perception as refugees from modernity is the theme which most clearly unifies New Age Travellers, this group is extremely diverse. New Age Travellers do not form *a* community, but rather an amalgamation of diverse ethnicities (such as Irish, Spanish, German, Dutch, American, French, Italian, as well as English) and aesthetic or counter-cultural impulses (60s hippie, 70s punk, 80s grunge, and 90s rave). When asked what name they preferred to call themselves, several chose simply *Travellers*, a gesture of solidarity with Irish Travellers whose caravan lifestyle they admire and emulate. Others similarly chose to take on the name *Travellers* instead of *New Age Travellers* in order to dissociate themselves from any strong connection with the New Age movement, perceiving it as far too esoteric and ideologically confused. However, this name glosses over important distinctions between Irish Travellers and New Age Travellers, and masks periodic conflicts which emerge when, for instance, the former perceive that the latter are caricaturing their way of life. These antagonisms will perhaps in the future be exacerbated by the potential competition between these two communities for halting sites. Other New Age Travellers thought that attempts to *name* themselves, to impose a unifying label on such a diverse and vibrant community ran counter to the fundamental meaning of the New Age Traveller lifestyle itself. This New Age Traveller refusal of labels represents an attempt to resist the process of naming that would categorise, order, define or contain them. If a part of the project of modernity is to impose an order on disorder, to organise chaos through the process of naming, organising, categorising (as Zygmunt Bauman[1] claims), the New Age Traveller refusal to be labelled is indicative of their more general critique of modernity.

Anti-modernity as lifestyle

What makes the New Age Traveller lifestyle unique and interesting is not simply that it is a celebration of chaos, of

---

1 Zygmunt Bauman, *Modernity and ambivalence.* Oxford: Blackwell Press, 1991

disorder, of the unruly, but rather that it represents an attempt at turning a critique of modernity into a way of life. As well as rejecting the process of labelling, New Age Traveller life is an explicit rejection of the organisation of space and time underpinning the modern household. The New Age Traveller advocacy of (geographical and spiritual) nomadism is a rejection of the notion of the permanent habitat and of a stable identity that has played a crucial role in processes of modernisation. Since the mobility of New Age Traveller life and the practice of living in *single-room* shacks, tepees, vehicles, precludes the possibility of modern sanitation, the Traveller's life opens up the possibility of life without modern conveniences. Although many Travellers I spoke with managed to stay scrupulously clean (contrary to the *crusty* image of dirt and dreadlocks), their refusal to acquiesce in the contemporary fetish of the *bathroom* is an implicit rejection of the modern obsession with sanitation. Furthermore, their innovative, multi-functional living spaces are an implicit challenge to the fragmentation of the house into specialised rooms; into bathrooms, bedrooms and kitchens, within which individual bodies are fed, cleaned, regenerated and reproduced to the tempo of the working day. More generally, the multi-functional spaces which comprise New Age Traveller homes, the spatial and temporal (dis)order of their lifestyle, pose a challenge to the spatial and temporal ordering central to work and home life that is a part of the civilising and moralising processes of modernity.

Another feature unifies the diverse New Age Traveller communities and sets them apart from the broader community: their attitude and relationship to the formal economy. Although some New Age Travellers work for wages or even own small businesses, work within an informal economy (such as the LETS program in which skills are traded), or operate in an alternative economy (such as vending or juggling), many subsist by collecting the dole. For some, *dropping out* was a response to the meaninglessness they experienced in their previous jobs or professions. For instance, some expressed reluctance to participate in reproducing a system they perceived as based on an exploitative division of labour. Others preferred not to participate in what they viewed as an unethical system designed to create false needs. Still others were disillusioned with the alienation, the lack of autonomy they endured in their jobs or professions where they experienced themselves as an "appendage to the machine". Thus, the reluctance some expressed to participate in the formal economy was generally not based on an unreflexive desire to "freeload", but at times represented a thoughtful, reflexive ethical position based on a critique of exploitation, commodity fetishism and alienation.

New Age Travellers are often criticised by the broader community for their lack of participation in the formal economy. In my experience, New Age Travellers have been characterised as "parasites" and "freeloaders", as "wasters" and as "knackers". This anxiety expresses a very legitimate concern that the already overstretched welfare state cannot withstand more strain. However, the vehemence with which some of these negative sentiments are expressed indicate that New Age Travellers are sometimes feared and disliked not because of the potential drain on the welfare state, but because of the possibility that they will further destabilise traditional values already eroded by modernity. In a sense, some of the critiques of their potential drain on the welfare state are merely giving a rational, economic veneer to a more generalised fear of difference, change and diversity.

The references to New Age Travellers as "spongers" highlight one aspect of the moral economy underpinning anti-New Age Traveller sentiments: the notion that participation in gainful employment is a part of one's moral obligation to the community. In contrast, the moral economy underpinning New Age Traveller life is not based on one's relationship to production, but is more related to consumption. Unlike members of the broader community, New Age Travellers do not define *work* exclusively as participation in the formal economy. Rather, what makes New Age Traveller life unique, what unifies this diverse community is its commitment to living off the waste, the leftover, the excess of modernity.

For example, several New Age Travellers I spoke with diligently scoured dumps for material for clothes, furniture, kitchen appliances, or other household utensils, a practice they called "seagulling". Moreover, some of the more *settled* Travellers used this refuse to create makeshift homes out of tepees, rusty lean-tos, self-made shacks, abandoned vehicles. Some even routinely searched supermarket rubbish bins for fruit, vegetables, and even bags of thrown-out food from the deli counter, although apparently supermarket employees had taken to the habit of dying food unpalatable colours, such as blue, to discourage this practice. Thus, many New Age Travellers do not *work* in the formal sense, or do not engage in paid labour, but rather see their *work* as making the unusable usable, the unproductive productive. In short, they make a vocation, a lifestyle, out of living off the excess of modernity.

Living a lifestyle oriented towards making the unproductive productive, the unusable usable, inverts the conventional economy that gives priority to one's relationship to production. Relocating this moral imperative, this ethical responsibility, in the realm of consumption rather than production, reconceptualising collective responsibility in terms of waste, not wages, can be seen as a legitimate and principled value on which to base a lifestyle. The extent to which New Age Traveller life is oriented to finding innovative if laborious ways of reviving various *dead* objects of modernity is particularly apparent on Cúl (*Cool*) mountain, a New Age Traveller community near Dunmanway in West Cork. A number of New Age Travellers have *settled* in this community for as long as twelve years, setting up homes in sparse, eclectic, and imaginative habitats out of a broad variety of materials: an old ambulance, a tourist information booth, a makeshift tepee made out of plastic bags. Although their primary orientation to such refuse is functional, some of these habitats ironically signify those very aspects of modernity that many Travellers are trying to escape, such as the *panic* culture symbolised by the ambulance, the commodification of nature symbolised by the tourist information booth, the environmental crisis of industrial society signified by the non-biodegradable plastic bags. As such, the political economy of New Age Traveller life is based on living off the waste of others, and establishing a principled relationship to the global community.

The paradox of modernity

Thus, the New Age Traveller life strongly illustrates the paradox of modernity which on the one hand provides us with the illusion of the possibility of retreat, but on the other is unable to deliver its utopian promise. On the one hand, Travellers on Cúl mountain are utopian, for they conceive of the quiet rural life they lead on the mountain as in one sense a refuge from modernity. On the other hand, the Cúl mountain people are realists. By making the unusable usable and the unproductive productive, they acknowledge the worst aspects of modernity and try to tackle this problem head-on. This experience of being caught between two worlds, the utopian and the real, was also apparent in their own feelings of being caught between their old lives and their new lives. For instance, several claimed they felt torn between the lives they had literally carved out on the mountain, and the lives they left behind; they felt ambivalent about staying and ambivalent about leaving. Thus mountain life is much more than a nostalgic retreat to a rural, mythical, agrarian past. Rather, this life expresses both a longing for the premodern, the traditional, the refuge from modernity, and at the same time the recognition that there is really no refuge, no utopia, no place outside modernity where one can hide.

... excluding ...

CHAPTER 15

Irish Travellers and the Logic of Genocide

ROBBIE MCVEIGH

I n 1995 and 1996 a number of controversial public statements were made about Irish Travellers. These coincided
with a widespread alarm about crime, particularly
violent crime, in the south of Ireland. The issues dovetailed
as Travellers began to be held responsible for the perceived
new crime wave. This development was strikingly similar to
earlier "moral panics" about crime. In the book *Policing the
Crisis,* Stuart Hall and others[1] developed the concept of moral
panic to provide a powerful analysis of the process whereby
particular ethnic groups are used to exemplify a perceived
breakdown in law and order. In much the same way, the
existence of Travellers became emblematic of failures and
tensions surrounding crime within Irish society in 1995-6.

The moral panic

The moral panic relating to Irish Travellers, however, had a
further dimension which is also sociologically significant.

---

1   S. Hall, C. Critcher, T. Jefferson, J. Clarke and B. Roberts, *Policing
the crisis: mugging, the State, and law and order*, London: MacMillan,
1978

The process of blaming Travellers was not simply an example of stereotyping or racism. At the heart of Irish anti-Traveller scapegoating is a logic which is not just discriminatory – it is *genocidal*. Genocide, a word which derives from the Latin words *genus,* meaning a group, and *caedere,* meaning to kill, was coined after the Second World War. One of the first matters taken up by the new United Nations General Assembly in 1946 was the prevention and punishment of the crime of genocide. A *Genocide Convention* was ratified by the Assembly in 1948. This convention confirms that genocide is a crime under international law, recognises that humanity has suffered great losses from this crime, and states that international cooperation is necessary to liberate humankind from it. It defines the crime of genocide as:

> ... any of the following acts committed with intent to destroy, in whole or in part, a national, ethnical, racial or religious group, as such: (a) killing members of the group; (b) causing serious bodily or mental harm to members of the group; (c) deliberately inflicting on the group conditions of life calculated to bring about its physical destruction in whole or in part; (d) imposing measures designed to prevent births within the group; or (e) forcibly transferring children of the group to another group.

Thus it is possible, in international law, to see genocide as not just about killing a group of people but also about creating and reproducing and tolerating *social conditions* which might end their continued existence as a separate group. Moreover, I want to suggest that much Irish anti-Traveller rhetoric carries with it an inherent *genocidal logic* – that is, it exhorts government to act towards Irish Travellers in ways which can be interpreted as coming within the definition of genocide of the United Nations Genocide Convention. If settled people do not want Travellers to be given *either* halting sites *or* housing, then they do not want them to exist at all. They may not say "we don't want Travellers to exist" but the *logical implication* of their attitudes is that Travellers should not exist as a separate group.

This concern with the logic of genocide connects very directly with recent work by Zygmunt Bauman in *Modernity and the Holocaust*. His thesis is that existing analysis of the Holocaust has constructed it as a uniquely terrible atavistic phenomenon when in fact it was a consequence of modernity. He argues that the Holocaust was born and executed in our modern rational society, at the high stage of our civilisation and at the peak of human cultural achievement. Moreover, the project was *utopian;* it was based on the notion that modernity gives us the means to create a new and better society:

> Modern genocide is genocide with a purpose. Getting rid of the adversary is not an end in itself. It is a means to an end ... The end itself is a grand vision of a better, and radically different, society.[2]

Nomadism as failure of modernisation

This thesis has immediate resonance when we look at contemporary discourse about Travellers in Ireland. Genocidal logic is not the preserve of the extreme right; it emanates from journalists, public office holders and representatives of all the major political parties in Ireland. Moreover, the existence of Travellers is very often identified as key evidence of failure of the modern Irish state to address its social problems. There is nothing unusual in this. Around the world, the continued existence of nomadic peoples has become a motif for the failure of the modernisation project. It is assumed that nomadism and modernisation are inherently incompatible and that the only way to offer the supposed benefits of modernity to nomads is to end their existence as a distinct

---

2   Z. Bauman, *Modernity and the Holocaust*, Oxford: Polity Press, 1991, p 91

group. In consequence, the logic of genocide underpins not only the approach of those people who are violently anti-nomad but also those who want to help.

Whether the rhetoric is couched in terms of kindness to the nomad or sedentary necessity, the solution is always the termination of nomadism. The nomad is increasingly caught in this genocidal dialectic between sympathetic incorporation and unsympathetic repression. Genocide and assimilation carry with them the same ruthless imperative: the relentless sedentary colonisation of nomadic space.[3] So the logic of genocide is not the preserve of people who "hate" Travellers; it is also implicit in the work of people and organisations who have sought to *support* Travellers in different ways.

Media rhetoric

The discussion about Irish Travellers was re-opened by an intervention from the restaurant critic Helen Lucy Burke :

> I believe that some cultures are more respectable than others. Skip to the ramshackle collections of rusting cars, ramshackle caravans, mangy dogs, snotty-nosed children and women looking twenty years older than their actual age. This is part of their "culture" and they hold to it. People who claim to speak for them declare it is their right not just to live as they choose but to be supported and encouraged in their way. For years the Travelling People gave us to understand that they are exactly the same as the rest of us, but with caravans. Now some claim that they are a separate race and ethnic group. This is incorrect: their names, race, features are Irish. Their language, Shelta, is a form of backslang or Thieves' Cant, done through the medium of Irish. They

---

3 R. McVeigh, "Theorising sedentarism: the roots of anti-nomadism" in T. Acton (ed), *Gypsy politics and Traveller identity,* University of Hertfordshire Press, 1997

say little about respecting the culture and sensibilities of their settled neighbours ... Proponents of the "respect for all cultural traditions" school of thought seem to have no difficulty in squaring their beliefs with the rights of the weak within the culture. There is even a school of thought *condemning what the Spanish did to the Aztecs in Mexico*, destroying that wonderful old culture. The neighbours of Aztecs saw it in a different light, having endured the old traditions of flaying, roasting, having their living hearts torn out, and being eaten. *This is carrying the logic to an extreme*, and not for one moment do I suggest a parallel in Travellers' customs. But their social traditions within their families do not respond well to scrutiny, strongly resembling some African tribal customs where women are treated like pack-animals. (*Sunday Tribune*, 2 April 1995, my emphasis)

Helen Lucy Burke in this piece comments on history, anthropology and sociology. Her intervention recalls the stereotypes of many *ordinary* settled people. In expressing such views she opened a debate which was prevented by the silence of many settled people who think and act in terms of such stereotypes about Travellers and yet never give expression to them in public. It is characteristic of a moral panic that it normalises prejudice; it brings forth those things which "just have to be said".

Burke's intervention seemed to make it okay to think the unthinkable, to say the unsayable: to thrust off the unbearable fetters of *political correctness* and speak with an open mind on the *Traveller problem*. Travellers' disadvantage was explained in terms of pathologising Traveller culture and the main priority became getting rid of this "less respectable" culture through sedentarisation, assimilation or other strategies carrying a genocidal logic. This kind of approach was brought into even sharper focus by further written attacks on Travellers. Soon all the *respectable* Irish newspapers were filled with headlines such as, "Travellers' mafia preys on elderly" and "Long history of attacks by small gangs of Travellers on old people in rural areas". The moral panic even crossed the Atlantic as an article on "The Travelling Thugs" in the *Irish Voice* in the USA. An article by Mary Ellen Synon, described Traveller lifestyle under the banner headline, "Time to get tough on tinker terror 'culture'". She expounded on the nature of Traveller identity as follows:

> It is a life of appetite ungoverned by intellect. It is a life which marauds over private property and disregards public laws. It is a life of money without production, land without cost, damage without compensation, assault without arrest, theft without prosecution, and murder without remorse. It is a life worse than the life of beasts, for beasts at least are guided by wholesome instinct. Traveller life is without the ennobling intellect of man or the steadying instinct of animals. This tinker "culture" is without achievement, discipline, reason or intellectual ambition. (*Sunday Independent*, 28 January 1996)

Since Traveller culture is so clearly without merit in this analysis, there can be no question that it should be accorded the dignity of being recognised as an ethnicity. Instead, this kind of theory is more likely to lead to further verbal attacks. Such attacks did come, from north and south of the border, with references to the need for shotguns and to "parasites and leeches" in society; interventions in the north applauded the hard stance taken south of the border.

There are a number of points about the succession of statements which were made about Irish Travellers. They are full of factual inaccuracies. It is no more appropriate to make such generalisations about *all* Travellers than it would be about *all* settled people. In this context it is particularly shocking to see politicians of any persuasion attacking one of the most socially excluded groups in Ireland. Making political capital out of attacking particular ethnic groups, however, is commonplace: a *moral panic* always works in a directly political way. As Hall *et al* pointed out, it focuses popular concern about crime in a particularly reactionary way and becomes a key element in *authoritarian populism*, mainly by creating a popular demand for reactionary and draconian law and order measures. Once the argument has been made that Travellers are "parasites" or "leeches", the implications do not have to be spelt out.

A *product of modernity*

The key point about this is that these interventions were made by *respectable* journalists and politicians in *respectable* newspapers. It is striking that this kind of intervention appears in Ireland amid a homogeneous and consensual society, with no history of colonising other peoples, with a hegemony of christian democratic and social democratic politics. Bauman's thesis that genocide, far from being an example of atavistic primordial evil, is a product of modernity characterised by a rational bureaucratic approach to re-organising society, does seem relevant.

In this sense, the moral panic of 1995-6 was not without antecedents. The anti-Traveller public statements drew on a history of genocidal logic, which had already informed public opinion. For decades, dominant opinion in Ireland had accepted that there was nothing wrong with the principle of *getting rid* of Travellers. In the 1960s, the *pro-Traveller* Itinerant Settlement Movement made this explicit in its very name. The aim was assimilation and the disappearance of Travellers and Traveller culture. The only way to help Travellers was to destroy them. Moreover, in 1960, the Irish Government *Commission on Itinerancy* could quite happily identify sedentarisation and assimilation as the *solution* to the Traveller problem.

At the time of Helen Lucy Burke's comments, Traveller activists Nell and Michael McDonagh responded by warning of the connection between such *frankness* and the practice of anti-Traveller violence. They also made clear the connection which they saw between her thoughts on Traveller culture and earlier genocidal practice:

Helen Lucy Burke talked about hers being a superior culture. Does she not remember that this was what Hitler believed when he tried to wipe out the Gypsies as well as the Jews? ... Middle class people who come out with these things should realise that there are warped people out there only looking for encouragement to lob a petrol bomb into a trailer. We have been campaigning for twenty years for Travellers' rights. We worry greatly for future years, for our children. We could take you by the hand and bring you to Travellers who you could trust with your life. There's others you wouldn't want to meet. The same could be said for the settled people. We have been walked on all our lives, and you act like you have a God-given right to walk on us. You don't. This country would be a dull place if everyone was the same. Can we not celebrate diversity? (*Sunday Tribune*, 2 April 1995)

As we have seen, Helen Lucy Burke's intervention was followed by a deluge of anti-Traveller sentiment. The moral panic engineered around Irish Travellers and crime became a defining moment in relations between sedentary people and Travellers. Ireland is now a country in which the logic of genocide has taken root .

... modern responsibility ...

CHAPTER 16

Just Two Will Do

TANYA CASSIDY

O ver the last thirty years or so, Ireland has gone through tremendous social and economic changes. During this time, alcohol consumption has considerably increased as has car ownership. For instance, there has been more than a tenfold increase in the number of proceedings for drink-driving since 1960. In fact, these figures seem to increase sharply during summer bank holidays and at Christmas time, when more intense social activity takes place. Furthermore, we are regularly reminded of the potentially devastating effect of drinking and driving, through media campaigns and more sustained policing. Garda checkpoints have become a familiar feature of the festive season. But this has not happened smoothly. The public response to the problem of drinking and driving crystallises in many ways some essential features of the dynamic of modernity in Ireland.

Legal provisions

Legal provisions against being in charge of a vehicle while drunk have existed in Ireland for well over a hundred years, but it was the Road Traffic Act 1933, which introduced a new offence of drink-driving. It also put forward a legal definition of drunkenness, arguably a "very indefinite" one. One can only guess at the depth of dismay that such a legal definition provoked within a culture which placed drinking at its core and at the same time viewed "drunkenness" as an inability to hold one's drink. Drunkenness was perceived not as the normal outcome of drinking too much, but as the failure to behave appropriately. The very idea of a universal measure of drunkenness was also questioned; it was argued that the so-called "American idea of a blood test for alleged drunken drivers" discounted individual differences.

The explicit debate, however, revolved around the question of the powers of the "Guards which might be misused". This debate was revived by the Road Traffic Act 1961 which was branded as removing individual liberties. It was asserted that blood, urine or breath tests could raise "serious constitutional questions relating to personal rights" (*Dáil Éireann Reports* 1961: 412). One may recall that the dominant social philosophy in Ireland, mainly upheld by the Catholic Church, was antagonistic toward what was perceived as state intrusion in familial and individual lives. This kind of philosophy provided a convenient basis for hindering any serious enforcement of the rule against drink-driving.

One can nonetheless detect, at this stage, the beginning of a shift of attitude. In these same debates, Eamonn de Valera made a statement that foreshadowed the contemporary approach:

> We must not forget that the person who undertakes to drive a car while under the influence of drink is assuming a very serious responsibility vis-a-vis the rest of the community in that, by his very action, he is taking a risk that may have fatal consequences which he need not take. (*Dáil Éireann Report* 1961:454)

It is the individual who chooses to drink and drive who is responsible, and de Valera went on to say that "one does not need to be drunk to be a danger."

The Road Traffic Act 1968 introduced the blood-alcohol concentration (BAC) as absolute proof of an offence of drinking and driving. The level of alcohol was set at a fairly high level, 125 milligrams, which allowed for "normal" social drinking to take place. But the writing was already on the wall, as the relevant Minister argued at the time that "world opinion" had recently "moved sharply against the drinking driver" (*Dáil Éireann*, 1967:58).

The Road Traffic (Amendment) Act 1978 introduced roadside breathalising by the Gardai, and lowered the BAC to 100 milligrams. As it was pointed out at the time, "two-and-a-half pints of beer will put them beyond the statutory limit" (*Dáil Éireann Report* 1978: 2026). Not only was the drinking limit lowered, but the enforcement of the rule was considerably strengthened. Proceedings for drink-driving offences doubled after the introduction of the 1978 Act, reaching an all-time high, over twelve times the figure for 1961. The intolerance towards drink-driving had considerably increased. The drunk-driver who wilfully maimed and murdered was to be held totally responsible. But for that to happen, a complete transformation of drinking practices had to take place. The sociable drinker who conformed to fairly rigid rules of drinking had to be replaced by a more flexible drinker. In 1983, a deliberate move in that direction was initiated with the introduction of the "Just Two Will Do" campaign.

The anti-drink-driving campaigns

Supported by the drink industry, the "Just Two Will Do" campaign was launched by the Minister for the Environment (and Tanaiste) Dick Spring, who said "If everyone limited themselves to a maximum of two drinks when driving, the saving of lives and injuries would be enormous." The Wine and Spirits Association and the Irish Brewers' Association distributed half a million drip mats to pubs throughout the country to remind drivers to stick to the "Two Drinks" rule. In addition, posters were distributed to companies and premises which might hold functions involving alcohol over the holiday season. Finally, an all-round media campaign began using advertisements such as that shown below.

DRIVING ...?

The best time to decide about drinking and driving is before you go out!

How much can I drink without going over the limit?

It depends on a number of factors — for example, your weight, whether you have just eaten or are taking medicine. But if you stick to the "two-drinks" rule it is almost impossible to go over the legal blood/alcohol level for driving.

What if I go over the limit?

On conviction, you will automatically lose your licence for at least one year. So your job could be gone too if it depended on having a licence. You can now be fined up to £1,000 for a first offence.

What if they press me?

A real friend won't ask you to break the "two-drinks" rule. So don't spoil your own fun and everyone else's.

If you're driving...
Just two will do!

National Road Safety Association

This advertisement pointed out that there are numerous factors involved in the determination of how much one can drink without going over the legal limit. It also claimed that the two-drinks rule made it almost impossible to go over the limit. The "Just two will do" slogan captured the sociability of drinking in Irish society; at the time it would have been difficult to imagine that an individual could take a drink in the evening, without joining in and reciprocating. In this way, the two-drinks rule represented a realistic minimum. The campaign was then accommodating a central feature of traditional drinking in Ireland. As one of my informants in Cork City once told me "You never go out for just a pint in Ireland; even if you're only drinking with one other person, you each buy a round, so the least you drink is a quart".

In 1992, the National Safety Council (NSC) received, in addition to its regular grant from the Department of the Environment, an endowment of £500,000 for its Road Safety section from the Irish Insurance Federation. This grant meant that the Council was able to afford television advertisements for the first time, and two commercials were produced that year. A particularly gruesome one called *The Tap* depicted a pair of male hands being washed under a running tap of water. The washing hands turned over to expose blood-stains in the palms, and the commercial faded to black where the slogan "Drink-Driving. Forget it, or you never will" appeared. The other commercial produced that year by the NSC was the first version of the now "famous" Red Blanket commercial. This commercial depicted numerous bodies covered in red blankets stretching into the distance along a black tarmac road.

In 1995 this commercial was re-released, but the voice was replaced with a hauntingly plaintive melody in the background, and captions appeared at the bottom of the red blanket-covered bodies:

If you drink and drive
If you drive dangerously
If you speed

will you ever be able
to rest in peace?

This was followed by the legend STOP THE BLOODY SLAUGHTER in bold red letters.

The advertisement appealed to the consciences of the viewers, to the feeling of anticipated guilt at the very idea of being responsible for an accident or death. But the message was quite different to the one put across in the 1987 advertisement. The rule was now clear and did not make any allowance for the communal nature of drinking in Ireland. It is as if the authorities had abandoned the prospect of drinking moderation which would keep drivers below the limit. The message now was that if you chose to drink, you must find other means of transportation or that, if you wanted to drive, you must drink non-alcoholic beverage.

This campaign relied on a new perception, or perhaps promoted a new kind of individual drinker: the reflexive drinker. Such drinkers could now monitor their own behaviour and decide on what to drink and how much, according to the situation they found themselves in. The driver within a group would have to curtail severely his or her own drinking, and would be in a sense excused by the group. Pressure would not be exercised on this individual to drink more, to "have another one". The drinking of non-alcoholic drink would not bring derision.

Underlying all of these messages was the notion that one should never drink and drive. In fact, this became more explicit with the introduction of the Road Traffic Act 1994, which stiffened penalties, and lowered the BAC to 80 mg. The following appeared on all sides of Eastern Health Board ambulances and vehicles, as part of their health awareness:

NEVER
EVER (both in bold red lettering)
DRINK + DRIVE (in black)

This message was directed at the modern, civic-minded individual, one who had rejected the traditional Irish drinking culture. Or rather it promoted the emergence of such an individual.

Drink-driving as a problem

An American sociologist, Joseph Gusfield, argues that there are two main components involved in the analysis of the drink-driving issue: responsibility and ownership. Responsibility involves both drink-drivers and those charged with dealing with the problem at the political level. Ownership of the problem implicates those groups which acknowledge having a stake in the issue, but also those who disown the issue. "The concept of 'ownership of public problems'" says Gusfield, "is derived from the recognition that in the arenas of public opinion and debate all groups do not have equal power, influence, and authority to define the reality of the problem".[1] Specifically, he says that ownership refers to the ability to "create and influence public definition of a problem". The ownership of the issue of alcohol is contested between the anti-alcohol lobbies, often backed by the medical or scientific communities, and the drink industry. The former supports an anti-alcohol position and is generally rooted in ascetic attitudes which have originally been propagated by temperance or prohibition movements. The other approach has been traditionally identified with the alcohol industry.

In terms of the specific issue of drinking and driving, this problem has been clearly taken over by one side and disavowed by the other side. The public authorities could not avoid taking responsibility for pubic safety on the roads, and consequently they had to address the issue of drink-driving which constitutes a significant cause of road accidents and deaths. They took ownership of this problem, but they went a long way to accommodate traditional drinking practice in

---

1 Joseph Gusfield, *The culture of public problems: drinking-driving and the symbolic order*, Chicago: The University of Chicago Press, 1981, p 10

Ireland. They allowed at first for high tolerance drinking, repressing only the most excessive forms of drink-driving. Then they adopted a position which allowed only for *moderate* drinking. At the end of this long process, the rule became absolute: no drink-driving. The punters in the pubs had to find their own way of living with this rule. This does not necessarily mean that drinking practices have changed.

All those associated with the production and sale of alcohol constitute the other social force implicated in the ownership of this public problem, with the passive support of those who actually do the drinking. The battle was fought on the issue of defining drunkenness, frequently presented as a personal flaw or weakness rather than an actual excess of drink. Then, the focus shifted to the issue of intrusive control and breach of individual rights. The problem was in many ways disowned by those who provide alcoholic drinks: drink-driving is not an issue of excessive drinking but of incompetent drivers. In other words, it was not their problem. However, they have in the recent past adopted a more positive attitude toward assuming some ownership of this problem and, for example, they have provided late-night transport for their customers. But the overall tendency has been to direct the responsibility for drink-driving at the driver and the ownership of this issue at the government.

Drink, modernity and ambivalence

Zygmunt Bauman has argued that modernity is founded on the elimination of ambivalence. Drink was bound to be the target of the modern project if, as Room[2] has argued, ambivalence remains the most widespread theme associated with the study of drinking issues. The history of anti-drink-driving in Ireland can easily be read as the modern attempt at removing the ambivalence which has long surrounded

---

2 Robin Room, "Ambivalence as a sociological explanation: the case of cultural explanations of alcohol problems", *American Sociological Review*, vol 41 (1976): 1047-65

drinking. This ambivalence manifested itself in a reluctance to define any kind of drinking as excessive and in attributing drunkenness not to the amount drunk, but to some personal flaw. Removing ambivalence meant that the individual, specifically the drinking driver, is considered to be fully responsible.

But despite the best efforts of public authorities, the ambivalence surrounding alcohol in Ireland is not removed. Underlying the issue of drinking and driving is the moral divide associated with alcohol. Modernity has been marked by the introduction of a moral and largely negative appoach to alcohol. From the latter part of the eighteenth century, alcohol (originally only whiskey) was viewed as the root of insanity, as well as the cause of many social ills. At the same time, there was large-scale expansion in the alcohol industry. Commercial enterprises promoted the more positive, communal aspects of drinking. Modern debates about drinking are still conducted in terms of an opposition between the so-called *wets* and *drys*, and this sustains the inherent ambivalence of drinking issues.

But there exists another source of continuing ambivalence. Individuals are not likely to behave according to the clear imperatives which have been formulated by public authorities. There are continued ambiguities regarding the issue of consumption of alcohol. More importantly, however, the sociability of drinking is intimately linked to the Irish pub culture; ritual drinking practices such as rounds-buying still feature prominently, although there seems to have been changes in these areas in most recent times. Bauman urges that it is now time for a reconciliation with ambivalence and that we have to learn how to live in an uncurably ambivalent world.[3]

---

3 Zygmunt Bauman, *Modernity and ambivalence*, Cambridge: Polity Press, 1991, p 231

... the wastes of modernity ...

CHAPTER 17

"Rubbish"

MICHEL PEILLON

I n a world of intensified production and induced consumption, what is discarded and rejected grows to enormous proportions. Advanced capitalist societies nowadays accumulate rubbish. Serious minds are addressing this issue as a matter of urgency and the management of waste represents a crucial undertaking. The Commission of the European Union has engaged in a major review of the strategic disposal of waste. Levies and incentives are suggested as a means of reducing Europe's growing waste mountains.

Ireland has now joined the league of heavy rubbish producers. It faces in this respect problems for which it is not mentally prepared. The Minister for the Environment has in 1995 successfully passed a Waste Bill, meant to reduce the production of waste as well as exercise more control over its disposal. Anti-litter campaigns are regularly launched by the minister, with little effect. County councils busily prepare plans for future waste disposal; they desperately try to identify sites for waste dumping which will generate the least opposition and upheaval.

Dumping domestic waste

The problem is getting worse. Ireland ranks as one of the worst offenders in terms of coastal pollution. Marine waste is increasing at an alarming pace. Barely treated sewage continues to be poured into rivers and sea. More and more land must be set apart for *super-dumps*. Litter damages the image of Ireland as a clean holiday destination. The disposal of industrial hazardous waste raises many more anxieties. What to do with rubbish has long ceased to constitute a mere technical problem of planning and management. Local residents have intervened to make sure that it becomes a central public issue. They have shown great determination in opposing the dumping of "rubbish" near them and they continue to create serious difficulties for public authorities. Local communities are not concerned with the national or global issues of waste disposal, but with the proximity of rubbish to their own locality. Space becomes highly politicised when waste is to be dumped into it.

The reluctance to get close to that which has been rejected as waste simply derives from the fact that it is treated as dirt. All societies include within their mental map a category of dirt, to which are assigned diverse materials and practices. The anthropologist Mary Douglas has contended that dirt is simply matter which is out of place. It stands as an offence against order, as disorder. She points to the daily battle which is fought, in each home, against dirt. "In chasing dirt, in papering, decorating, tidying, we are not governed by anxiety to escape disease, but are positively re-ordering our environment, making it conform to an idea".[1] Dirt refers to that which has no place in our classification, other than a thoroughly negative and residual one. In that sense, the label does not apply to the physical properties of objects, and dirt is not characterised by qualities which can be objectively defined; it indicates what is done with such objects. Some discarded items do not become rubbish: they are re-used and labelled *second-hand*. What is excrement to some becomes high-quality manure for others. In a fundamental sense, an

---

1   Mary Douglas, *Purity and danger. An analysis of concepts of pollution and taboo*, London: Routledge and Kegan Paul, 1966, p 2

object becomes rubbish by being dumped or on its way to the dump site. Therefore, the dump sets the scene for a *rite of passage* through which something useless is branded as rubbish.

But dirt should not simply be perceived in this context as a residual category. It brings danger when "... it blurs, smudges, contradicts or otherwise confuses accepted categories".[2] We enter with dirt into a domain which exists beyond our sense of order, a world of serious transgressions which cannot be left unchecked. Dirt will for this reason prompt a range of behaviour which is best characterised as "anti-pollution behaviour". It aims at separating the pure and the impure, the clean and the soiled. This separation is achieved in a physical way, through the spatial movement of objects away from each other. It operates mainly by prohibiting contact with dirt, with the source of pollution. Through anti-pollution behaviour, the "purity" of the group is defended and reproduced.

Local residents all over Ireland have in the last few years initiated a type of behaviour which can be labelled anti-pollution behaviour. They have engaged in a struggle against impurity: against that which threatens the physical, cultural and social integrity of their collectivity. Ringsend residents in Dublin have mobilised a wide panoply of collective protests in their opposition to the construction of an incinerator at Pigeon House Road: marches, rallies, petitions. Candlelight vigils and vehicle cavalcades were also used to resist the erection of an incinerator at Clarecastle, near Ennis (County Clare). The plan for the construction of a sewage treatment plant at Mutton Ireland (Galway) triggered marches and counter-demonstrations, and their saga is still continuing.

Tipheads and landfill dumps, where discarded objects are concentrated in one spatial location, have in the last few years prompted much community action. Early in 1995, local

---

2 Mary Douglas, *Implicit meanings. Essays in anthropology*, London: Routledge and Kegan Paul, 1975, p 51

residents maintained a two-day picket at Dunsik city dump (Dublin) in order to force its closure. They were complaining about rats, smell and traffic: about the proximity of concentrated dirt. A few weeks later, a number of community councils staged a demonstration and blocked the traffic to have a plan for a super-dump near Blanchardstown scrapped. In 1996, major campaigns were under way to halt plans for new landfill dumps in the counties of Meath, Limerick and Wicklow. These should not be seen as some momentary outbursts of anger.

> Members of the Ballynagran and Coolbert Action Group held a party outside Wicklow County Council offices yesterday, to mark three years of picketing council meetings. The group is protesting against plans for a landfill dump of 300 acres of prime agricultural land south of Rathnew. They served minced pies and mulled wine to the councillors. (Adapted from the *Irish Times*, 10 December 1996)

Not everything which is discarded elicits anti-pollution behaviour. It depends on the degree of *rubbishness*, on how undesirable or repulsive dirt is perceived. Some rejects are used by other people and become simply second-hand. Then litter is strewn about in our most immediate surrounding. The organic waste which accumulates in tipheads rots away most unpleasantly. But a significant part of the municipal waste is not degradable and does not disappear. The repugnant sewage sludge and the threatening toxic pollution which comes from industrial waste form the most extreme kind of rubbish.

This classification covers a wide range of dirt, from the familiar to the most alien and threatening. In this scheme, culture is given as the source of rubbish, and the density of rubbishness is measured by its distance from *nature*. Pollution occurs when the sheer accumulation of cultural behaviour (such as the concentration of people in urban areas or in touristic centres) does not allow the natural processes to take care of domestic wastages and sewage. Excessive industrialisation and intensive agriculture continue to create the most serious pollution. Nowadays, packaging constitutes a high proportion of the twenty-two kilos of rubbish which are produced on average by each Irish household every week. It forms the cultural wrapping, the system of signification which is elaborated around the product. The substance is consumed or degrades naturally; the mainly synthetic wrapping remains after it has ceased to operate as commodified sign, after it has been separated from its substance. The different categories of dirt correspond to a mental map of the social world. Anti-pollution behaviour is triggered when the concentrated dirt gets physically close to us.

Social outcasts

A very physical kind of impurity destroys the environment and erodes the natural processes which sustain our human existence. But the category of dirt is not confined to physical objects. People too may be so labelled: "downs and outs", New Age Travellers, itinerant people, etc. Their campsites, which are inherently mobile and for this reason highly threatening, are perceived as locations where rubbish gathers and dirt accumulates. Mary Douglas dryly comments that "... the probability of being accused of pollution will fall on the paupers and second-class citizens of various types:[3] all those who inhabit the shadowy world where the models according to which life is ordered begin to slip away and disintegrate. The image that people have of Travellers is one commonly associated with "dirt" and "rubbish". The encampment of Travellers is seen to be strewn with rubbish and often lacks personal facilities; they deal with discarded industrial commodities; the personal appearance of many Travellers is construed in terms of dirt, especially the

---

3 Mary Douglas, *ibid*, p 240

children. In May 1996, residents living close to the Ballygoan tiphead (Dublin) organised a picket and prevented refuse lorries from emptying their loads. Their action was directed at the county council, which was accused of refusing to take the appropriate steps and compel Travellers to move away from the tiphead. Two perceived categories of dirt were cumulating in an explosive combination.

Through the years, communities of local residents have come together and engaged in anti-pollution behaviour directed at the Travellers. In January 1995, farmers in Enniscorthy (County Wexford) demonstrated against the presence of an itinerants' encampment and demanded their ejection from their temporary campsite. A few months later, several hundred residents at Moate (County Westmeath) blocked the main Dublin to Galway road to protest against the housing of a Travelling family: they asked for them to be rehoused "elsewhere". Toward the end of the same year, residents of Ballina (County Mayo) objected to the proposal by Mayo County Council to build a halting site for Travellers. The story of the attempt at settling itinerants in Dublin will have to be told one day. But one knows that every resident association is fiercely mobilised as soon as mention is made of a halting site or of an housing scheme for itinerants nearby. For this reason, very little progress has been made in solving the problems of Travellers.

Local residents are now most prone to collective protest. Independent Ireland has been imagined, from the very start, as a community of communities. And this idea has now come into being, but in a perverse way. Far from incarnating the public spirit, community has become the main medium for the denial of a public will. Community associations are upholding an egoism which draws its strength from its collective basis, without ever being able to claim the legitimacy of the public sphere. Local residents are no moral agents; they do not act according to general principles of what is right and wrong in the public domain. They do not seek the high ground of universalism. They probably accept that halting sites must be constructed: but not close to them.

They only offer a private solution which transfers the problem elsewhere. They are involved in anti-pollution behaviour, and it has nothing to do with taking a moral stance.

Anti-drugs protests

Community constitutes the intermediary space between the private and the public domains. It mediates between the confining warmth of privacy and the remoteness of the public sphere. In Ireland, the latter has acquired an external character: nobody's rather than everybody's domain. It can be vandalised and rubbish thrown in it. Yet, this no-man's-land is being reclaimed as communal domain.

> On 13 December 1996 (*Irish Times*), it was reported that an angry crowd of about five hundred people staged a noisy protest outside the home of an alleged drug dealer in a Dublin suburb. The protesters were mainly from the inner-city, Coolock and Darndale. They stood at the house shouting "scumbag, scumbag". A number of them rapped on the door and windows, setting off the burglar alarm. A handful of protesters climbed onto the porch and placed a mock coffin, reading: "Drugs kill". The crowd then turned to another house accross the road, where an associate lived. Its alarm was also set off and one of the crowd fired fireworks over the roof of the first man's house and into the back garden.

After a long sequence of protests, staged all through 1996 and accelerated in the autumn, protesters have turned to an explicit language of dirt: "Scumbag! Scumbag!". Their collective action aims at eliminating a source of pollution and represents anti-pollution behaviour. Pollution occurs when what is pure and unsoiled comes into contact with what is impure and soiled. The first form of anti-pollution behaviour aims at avoiding contact with impurity, at keeping off the potential source of pollution. This occured in October 1995, when Blanchardstown hospital planned to open a drugs clinic. It triggered an immediate reaction by local residents who organised rallies against such a proposal. They claimed that the drug clinic would attract a large number of drug addicts into their area and make the place less salubrious and less safe. The regular visiting of such people, who are widely perceived as *pariahs*, would threaten the social and cultural fabric of the area. Similarly, in the spring of 1996, a round-the-clock vigil was started in some West Tallaght housing estates. It consisted of local residents setting up makeshift tents in strategic positions on the green areas or in front of the homes of known local dealers. Women occupied the tents during the day and men took their turn throughout the night. The idea was to drive dealers out of the estates by starving them of business.

The second form of anti-pollution behaviour consists in forceful exclusion. In late February 1996, one hundred people converged on a flat in the Dolphin's House complex to force out an alleged drug dealer. The crowd gathered outside the man's home and demanded that his parents force him to leave. The man was slightly injured in the clash with the protesters; he subsequently left the area. This type of action has intensified all through the year. Typically, a large group of local residents organise a march which inevitably ends in front of the home of known drug dealers. It puts a great deal of pressure on known local dealers and makes life uncomfortable for them. It aims at rejection and eviction and does not hesitate to use force in its attempt to remove the source of pollution.

Communal identities and the fragmentation of modernity

In relation to waste, to Travellers and finally drugs, the community emerges as the main agency in the attempt to control and ultimately reject *dirt*. Like any group, community constitutes itself by what it includes and, even more so, by what it excludes. It does not define itself positively and reflexively, by articulating an identity according to which it coheres. Rather, it asserts its reality through what it rejects as dirt, as rubbish. Its "anti-pollution behaviour" clearly states what it considers to be undesirable, repulsive or threatening. It identifies those features which, it thinks, damage the quality of life for the collectivity. It points to those uncongenial elements which pose a threat to its normal mode of existence. Its identity is activated by what undermines it; its profile is sketched in the dirt, the impurity it rejects.

Alain Touraine[4] has registered the decline of those forces which dominated industrial society and which upheld universal values and goals such as wealth creation, progress and freedom. He observes instead a multitude of small-scale agents (ethnic groups, communities of lifestyle, neighbourhoods) intent on promoting their own identities. In the absence of a broader project of social transformation, such social agents prove themselves incapable of transcending their narrow self-interests, however legitimate they may be. The egoism of local communities in Ireland should be seen, then, as the outcome of the fragmentation which characterises late modernity.

---

4 Alain Touraine, *Critique of modernity*, Oxford: Blackwell, 1995